WHO'S YOUR Daddy NOW?

Doug Stringer

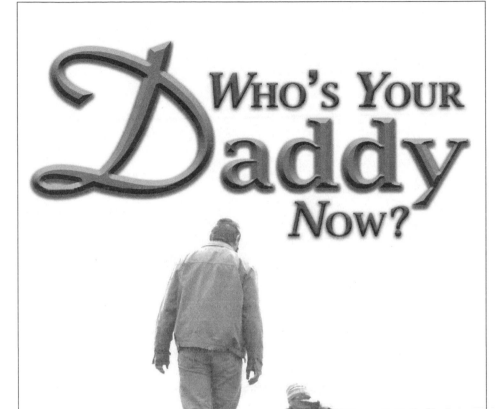

WHO'S YOUR Daddy NOW?

The Cry of a Generation
in Pursuit of Fathers

by Doug Stringer

gateKeeper
PUBLISHING

Published by GateKeeper Publishing LLC

Who's Your Daddy Now?

Copyright 2007
By Doug Stringer

ALL RIGHTS RESERVED

ISBN 10: 0-9704753-4-9
ISBN 13: 978-0-9704753-4-3

Published by
GateKeeper Publishing, LLC.
176 Sandbank Rd.
Cheshire, CT. 06410

Cover design by April Campbell
GateKeeper Publishing, LLC.
Permitted standard license for photography purchased
from istockphoto.com

DEDICATION

To Jeanne and Kenny, my younger sister and brother (always "little" sister and brother to me): At the lowest points of my life, thoughts of you and a sense of responsibility to be there for you are what kept me going. Our family had many challenges, but we were still a family nonetheless. Though Dad was your biological father and my stepfather, he saw no distinction. Both Mom and Dad were very proud of each of us. I cherish the memories we share of growing up together. I can still remember being nine, then ten years old when each of you were born and the exuberant joy of having a little sister and brother. Yes, I will always remember the cloth diaper days...before disposables were invented.

To Judy: You were always "daddy's girl" to your father — who was my biological father — and I know you miss him dearly. I pray that you would come to know you have a Heavenly Father who loves you even more and desires to hold that same place in your heart as our father held.

To my mom, my stepfather, and my biological father, who — by the grace of God — are now all with the Lord. Though growing up was not always easy, I cherish and honor the lessons I learned and the relationship we had as we grew to love one another even more through our adversities and challenges. In reality, I have so many fond memories, especially from our times together after we found a common place of healing in Christ.

To those who are literally my personal spiritual sons and daughters — Randy, JT, Andrew, Monica, John, Debbie, Bob, Scott, Dale, Julius, Melanie and so many more — and to all those who have adopted me as a father in the faith: What a pleasure it is, by God's grace, to walk this walk with you.

To those like myself who do not know how to be good spiritual parents: May God's grace be multiplied unto you as you learn to be fathers and mothers to an emerging generation.

And especially to an entire emerging generation in pursuit of spiritual fathers: May you receive a fresh revelation of your Heavenly Father and the destiny He has for you.

In Memory of Judge Tony Guillory

Judge Tony Guillory was a man of faith, a champion of courage, and a mighty man of God. He considered me one of his spiritual fathers, yet was also an example himself of the father's heart to those around him — though he never even knew his own father. He always found time for others and was often giving of his own time to speak to troubled youth.

Even though Tony was a man of stature in the community — working in Houston as an administrative judge for the EEOC — he was a man of great humility. He had once been assistant attorney general for the state of Texas, but many people didn't even know that because he was always more interested in listening to others than he was in talking about himself.

Tony put God first in all things. He took care of his family — his wife Vickie and their son Marquel. He brought wisdom and quiet strength to our board meetings. Even in the courtroom, those he ruled against still respected him because his judgments were just. He was part of our Mighty Men's ministry, a group of men who meet weekly to become better husbands, fathers, and men of God. He was a man who never had an unkind word to say about anyone.

Having walked with a limp for nine years following liver transplant surgery, one of Tony's greatest desires was to run again and to play ball with his son. Now, he is running once again in his glorified body! He ran ahead of us all, and he taught us how to triumph, even in adversity.

ACKNOWLEDGEMENTS

Thank you to Sarah and Janice for helping lay the foundation for this book by sorting and reviewing countless articles and video teachings; and to Belinda for your work in compiling, formatting and transcribing my "downloads." Also a special thanks to each of you who reviewed the preliminary manuscripts and provided your input, encouragement and examples.

"Doug clearly paints a picture of the role of a father in a child or teen's life and the effects that the absence of fathers are having on this generation. May the following pages inspire you to aggressively pursue and win your own children's hearts along with the hearts of those who are in need of a spiritual father to mentor and disciple them."

Ron Luce, President & Founder, Teen Mania Ministries

"*Who's Your Daddy Now?* will surely resonate strongly with anyone that has ever longed for the love of their natural father as well as anyone who has a heart to be a 'father' to those who need guidance. God has truly equipped Doug in a supernatural way to tear down the walls of this complex subject and to communicate God's truth in a practical yet biblically sound way. This book will be a necessary tool for equipping the Body of Christ and propelling us into a new place in God for generations to come."

Bishop Eddie L. Long, Senior Pastor, New Birth Missionary Baptist Church

"My friend, Doug Stringer, has written a powerful, prophetic masterpiece which will bring Our Master's peace into the hearts of fathers and children around the world! This timely and desperately needed book divinely bridges the gap between the generations and allows spiritual transfer for lasting spiritual legacy!"

Bishop Dale C. Bronner, D. Min., Senior Pastor and author,
Word of Faith Family Worship Cathedral

"Through Doug Stringer's book, God reveals His heart for a whole generation. I was challenged to see myself as a 'spiritual father' through whom God wants to invest into young lives. This book comes not just from Doug's life experiences, but it comes from the person God has molded Doug to be. He doesn't just write about investing in people, he lives it, giving *Who's Your Daddy Now?* amazing credibility and authority. Doug's communication style has always been 'straight talk with huge lashings of love.' He brings biblical examples to life to prophetically speak God's wisdom into both individual readers and into the culture. Definitely recommended reading."

Andrew Merry, Senior Pastor, Ocean Grove Fellowship, Geelong, Australia

"When I was asked to read the manuscript *Who's Your Daddy Now?* I had no idea it would touch a deep chord in my heart. From the stories Doug tells and through his amazing biblical insight, I was moved to tears, smiles, and even healing. I believe everyone will gain a closer relationship with the Father through the pages of this book. Thank you, Doug!"

Lisa Abbott, film producer & entertainment distributor

"This is a powerful and practical book that speaks to the heart concerning a subject that is on the cutting edge of our culture. Doug Stringer is wonderfully qualified to share tender, sensitive words that can bring healing and transformation to those who desire it. I recommend this book to all who are struggling with issues dealing with their fathers – and also for those who are not. Every reader will be challenged and blessed by this significant book."

Dr. Paul Cedar, Chairman, Mission America Coalition

"Doug's latest book is an insightful and meaningful one. He addresses the significance of fathers in the society, and most important, the pivotal role they play in shaping the values in our culture. He also raises the issue of the 'fatherless generation' that we are experiencing in the world today and its adverse effects on society. Doug gives the call for all men to rise up in true godliness and Christ-like character to affect change in our broken-down world today, beginning first with our families, then the church, then the world."

Kong Hee, Senior Pastor, City Harvest Church, Singapore

"Who's Your Daddy Now? is a handbook for fulfilling the destiny of two generations of fathers and sons: the Elijahs and the Elishas, the Pauls and the Timothys. Jesus didn't just disciple people, He trained them to think and function like apostolic servants. Doug's life is a testimony to an entire generation who don't fit in to the orthodox ways of American Christianity. It is Doug's passion for God and authentic love as an apostolic father that has pioneered a path for today's emerging leaders."

Matt Stevens, Director, Chain Reaction, Baltimore MD

"Wow! Talk about a book that makes you experience the whole spectrum! I went from a deep, aching in my heart and sadness for the state of our generation, then found myself wanting to jump up and down and say 'Here I am, send me!' Doug has done it again — his love for God and his heart for God's people shines brilliantly through this book. He loves us enough to be honest with us about our desperate situation but doesn't leave us scratching our heads over how to solve it. He provides the answers and the direction, based on God's Word, and presents it in such a wonderful and fresh way that every person can understand, no matter where they are on their spiritual journey."

Kimiko Soldati, U.S. Olympian

"This book reveals the need of a younger generation for leaders to journey with and a call to the elder generation to recognize we cannot reach our full potential without them. I love how Doug identifies the younger generation as different, but passionate for God's will and ready for an embrace of trust. Neither of the generations were ever meant to spread God's Kingdom separately or alone, but together."

Tony J. Fundaro, Lead Pastor, Life in Deep Ellum, Dallas TX

"Doug Stringer has come through personal pain into a place of victory, and God has commissioned him as a courageous and insightful instrument of healing for the fatherless — naturally and spiritually. His sensitivity in addressing this difficult subject demonstrates the Lord's tender compassion toward the abandoned and brokenhearted. This is not just a message Doug preaches and writes about; it is one he lives. He has earned the right to speak, and we should listen."

Brenda J. Davis, Editor, SpiritLed Woman

"I've known Doug Stringer and of his ministry for 25 years. There is much to be said about faithfulness and longevity. Doug's latest book *Who's Your Daddy Now?* will not only heal the relationship gulf between fathers and sons in the body of Christ - but also be the needle and thread that will sew the rip between fathers and sons in the secular world as well. As fathers, we must pass on a better world to our children. And in order to pass the baton to the next generation, we must be able to run along side them. In this latest book, Doug helps us to run with each other until it is time for our children to forge ahead. We have waited a long time to hear this message. Let the healing begin."

Dr. Ed Montgomery, author and pastor of
Abundant Life Cathedral Church, Houston, TX

"Who's Your Daddy Now? is so relevant to what is going on now in our world. I started reading it, and I couldn't put it down. I talk a lot about absent fathers in my ministry but I was still amazed with some of the statistics I read, and I've already been put in situations where I used what I read in Doug's book to minister to people. So often the church deals with the weeds but never deals with the roots. So many people have relationships with God the Father that are messed up because they don't have a relationship with their earthly father. I pray that people all over the world will read this message and will be convicted but also inspired. We need this book. It's life- changing!"

Melvin Adams, former Harlem Globetrotter

"Doug's new book *Who's Your Daddy Now?* is right on mark with what is happening in our culture. He has his finger on the pulse of the current condition of our generation. It's not a message of hopelessness and doom, but of hope and restoration. Doug's blend of God's truth and real-life stories makes for compelling reading and introspection. Thanks, Doug, for touching my heart and no doubt millions everywhere!"

Jay Mincks, Executive Vice President, Administaff

CONTENTS

FOREWORD BY REV. A. R. BERNARD SR.   17

INTRODUCTION   19

Part 1: WHO'S YOUR DADDY?

Who's Your Daddy?   29
Camels in the Wilderness   35
A Generation in Need   43
A Nation of Orphans   55

Part 2: WHERE DO DADDIES COME FROM?

Leading by Example   67
Daddies, Daughters, and Strength to Deliver   85
A Church God Can Use   101

Part 3: MY DADDY ROCKS!

The Rock of ALL Ages   117
The Father of All Nations   133
The Spirit of Adoption   145

Part 4: THAT'S MY GIRL! THAT'S MY BOY!

Honor and Blessing   163
Raising A Standard   179
Salty Christians   189

Part 5: Who's Your Daddy *Now*?

Dougie, Fix It?   199

Foreword

The sun shone brightly over the sky as the smell of a newly cut lawn filled the air. We all stood at attention as the casket draped in the American flag and led by a military honor guard came to rest at the grave site. How befitting a man who had contributed so much to a movement that called men to a place of decisiveness, strength, consistency and personal responsibility. He would say, "God has called me to speak with a prophetic voice to the men of this generation, that manhood and Christ-likeness are synonymous."

We all gathered to honor the memory of a man who touched us so deeply through his life and ministry. Family and friends stood teary-eyed as each stepped to the podium to share a testimony or offer their condolences to the family. But there were two families attending the funeral of Edwin Louis Cole that day. One of them was his blood family, the Coles and others. But there was also a family of men standing on the side in which he had filled a void in their lives by becoming their spiritual father. I was one of them.

It was my turn to be graced with the opportunity to say a few words. It was difficult to hold back the tears because he would be sorely missed by so many men like myself who saw him as a father. As I took the podium and began sharing my story, I looked at the Cole family and thanked them for sharing this man with us. But I also looked around at the men he fathered outside of his family. A prophetic realization rested upon me: It was time for those who were fathered to become fathers. I finished my brief presentation and returned to my seat feeling that a new season of men's ministry was dawning.

Among those spiritual sons fathered by Dr Cole was Doug Stringer. He took the message to heart. So I am not surprised that just a few years later he is releasing this book titled, oddly enough, *Who's Your Daddy, Now?*

I believe every man, father, pastor, youth leader, husband, son, and daughter should read this book. Doug not only raises the issue of fatherlessness which we are all too familiar with. But he sends out the clarion call to fill the void that was filled for us. It is a call to take responsibility for another generation looking for fathers to guide, guard, and govern their lives; to direct protect, and correct; to lead them into true manhood and true womanhood.

These words were written some 1900 years ago but they still apply today: *For though you may have ten thousand teachers in Christ, you do not have many fathers...* (1 Corinthians 4:15, New Century Version)

Thank you Doug, and congratulations!

-Rev. A. R. Bernard Sr., founder and senior pastor, Christian Cultural Center, Brooklyn NY

THE CRY OF A GENERATION

"There are times when I feel like the title 'father' is the worst name God could have given Himself. What a stupid idea, when 'father' means rejection in my world."

It was late Sunday night when I received this email message from "L." I had spoken that morning at a church we worked with during relief efforts for Hurricanes Katrina and Rita. My message was about God's love and mercy for the fatherless and His desire to adopt them into His own family. One of my board members was there, along with his sister.

This particular board member became addicted to drugs when he was a young man. His family asked me to help locate a full-time recovery regimen, so I helped him get into a Teen Challenge program directed by my friend Roger. Today, he runs the family business and heads up one of our Somebody Cares chapters. He has a beautiful family who all love the Lord.

All these years later, his sister's daughter is going through struggles of her own. It was she who sent the email and gave us permission to share what she wrote that night, in hopes of helping others:

> *I am 18 years old. I feel God pulling on my heart stronger than I'm comfortable with, so I'm doing what he told me to... writing to you. This is my story.*
>
> *Like my uncle, I'm extremely determined. The last two years of my life have been thorny to say the least. My dad left when I was 16, and ever since I've had a hard time trusting God. To be honest, there are times when I*

question His authority and even His existence. I live in a small two-bedroom apartment with my mom and 13-year-old brother, so the couch is my best friend.

Almost exactly a year ago I became pregnant. As you may know, I am adopted, as is my brother. I've always been immovably pro-life. I knew I had other options, I knew I was making a huge mistake; I knew what I was doing would destroy my spirit and tear out my heart, but I had an abortion six weeks later. I could make excuses as to why, but in reality we live with the choices we make.

I hate myself for that choice. The sound of the vacuum haunts my dreams to this day. I've just recently gotten to the point where I'm not ashamed of what I did. I don't try to hide it from people anymore. I want them to know so it doesn't happen to anyone else.

After the impact of what I had done hit me, I literally drank myself into a coma every night for about a year. I still struggle with alcohol periodically, but never really got into drugs, mainly because I didn't like them; however I know that if I had I would most likely be on the street at this point.

There are times when I feel like I've never really been loved by a hand that touched me. There are times when I feel like the title "Father" was the worst name God could have given Himself... what a stupid idea when the title "father" means "rejection" in my world. I guess I've been looking for something these last two years to justify my pain... to explain why all this has happened and why I am so screwed up.

I know that you can only find redemption through God and that no one can do it for you, but I usually stay away from people I'm angry with. Honestly, I want to go "Mike Tyson" on God most days.

Even though I've never met you, I have an obscene amount of respect for you and for what God did through you in my uncle's life.

I want to be who God wants me to be… and this isn't who God wants me to be… I want God to be proud of me. I want my family to be proud of me. I want to be proud of me.

I really appreciate you for taking the time to read my e-mail. I don't mean to dump all my problems on you or anything, I just felt like writing you was what God was telling me to do. I'd love to hear back from you.

With utmost respect, L.

Divorce, abandonment, rejection, pregnancy, abortion, alcohol, drugs—in one letter this young woman addresses many of the issues our fatherless generation faces daily, and they can all be traced back to a broken connection with a father. Her story echoes the heart-cry of an entire generation who only asked for the affirmation, acceptance, and approval of a father. What too many of them experienced, instead, was abandonment and absence. "L" says "father" means "rejection" in "her world," but she really speaks for an entire generation.

When I replied to the email, I told her no matter what she was going through or feeling, God the Father was there for her. I praised her for her honesty, because honesty is attractive to God. It's only in that place of vulnerability that He can begin to bring healing. I could tell she really wants to help others avoid the pain she has experienced, and I gave her hope that God would use her that way.

A few days later, I met with "L" in my office, and listened as she spoke openly from her heart. I let her know God wants to take what the enemy intended for evil and use it for her good. I told her God has a special love for those who are adopted. When she left, she had hope in her heart and joy on her countenance. She dreams of ministering someday to other young women who have experienced similar pain. In the meantime, she is receiving Christian counseling and reconciling with her family. Most of all, she is learning to accept God as her father.

What we have today is a "double generation" of fatherlessness, consisting of a former generation (mine) and an emerging generation that both grew up, for the most part, without fathers. Even those who have or had good fathers still suffer from the widespread effects of fatherlessness in our culture and our world.

But if God has added grace for the fatherless and for the widow, how much more grace will there be when an entire generation is fatherless? And if we now have a *double generation*, the former and the emerging, both termed fatherless, I believe we are going to see a *double portion of grace* poured out on these two generations who together will emerge as the "Gen-Edge miracle," a generation living on the edge of eternity. These generations will journey together to become the prophetic generation – meaning the generation spoken of by the prophets of old – rising up to prepare a people for the coming of the Lord!

Already we can see signs of this preparation. The Sentinel Group, producers of the "Transformations" video series, tracks lasting and sustained transformation in communities and nations throughout the world. In 1999, only eight cities were experiencing the kind of revival where every element of culture is touched. As a Sentinel Group board member, I can report that by early 2005 we knew of 350 cities worldwide—and even some nations— experiencing this level of revival.

This tells us God is doing something quickly, and He will not wait on those who sit back and stagnate in mediocrity and compromise. He's looking for a standard to be raised! We aren't called to be on the defensive—we should be proactively sharing the life of Christ to the next generation. We must be fathers and mothers to those emerging from life's wilderness, leading them to their Abba-Father through the Spirit of Adoption found in relationship with the Son of His love, Jesus Christ.

In the late 1980s, God began to give me insight regarding the state of our nation and the problems our ministry sees daily as we reach out to individuals struggling with drugs, alcohol, abortion, prostitution, apathy, and other issues. He revealed to me the root and source of all these issues: America is a nation devoid of fathers, both natural fathers and spiritual fathers. We are an orphaned nation with broken and dysfunctional families, a society of individuals in search of identity. Recognizing this, I began calling the emerging generation "the no-direction generation."

When I published this in my 1994 book, *The Fatherless Generation*, I didn't realize it would be even more relevant today, in 2006. Over a decade later – as I complete the manuscript for *Who's Your Daddy Now?* – the church is waking up to our need to "father and mother" a generation that has been abandoned and left to its own devices. And this is a worldwide condition, not one limited to our own country.

By the world's view, the emerging generation is merely one scattered in life's barren deserts. But God is calling them into their destinies! He is releasing a corporate sound of forerunners, preparing the way for the coming revival.

The prophets of old yearned to see the days in which we live; because the words God spoke through them are being fulfilled at *this* moment in time. This time it's not about one generation passing a baton to the next. God is a multi-generational God. He is simultaneously the God of Abraham, Isaac, and Jacob. He wants to release a multi-generational anointing on all who are willing. As He unites the wisdom and resources of former generations with the passion and zeal of the emerging generation, we become a synergistic force that is unstoppable in advancing the Kingdom of God!

At one of our meetings for emerging leaders, my friend Mike, a fellow minister of the Gospel at Somebody Cares Humble, Texas, echoed the passionate cries of our hearts with his closing prayer:

"There is a sound within this generation. We've heard the rumblings but we want to hear the full sound. Breathe on our minds, Lord, in areas where we have been wrestling to release this generation. Breathe on our hearts so we can see this generation come forth, so we can see this revival come to pass. We are sick and tired of the revival we only hear about. We want to see the revolution. Let the revolution begin!"

It is a cry of the heart, a corporate cry from a generation walking through the wilderness of life! It's a prophetic generation emerging from a double generation of the fatherless! It's a multi-generational anointing, calling forth the generations, the churches, and even the nations to come back to their Father!

The late Leonard Ravenhill wrote to me once: "My dearest brother Doug, let others live on the raw edge or the cutting edge… you and I should live on the edge of eternity."

On the edge of eternity, bringing in the harvest for the final days! That's the "Gen-Edge" miracle! I can think of no better place to be!

Are you ready and willing to be part of the journey?

Part I

Who's Your Daddy?

1

Who's Your Daddy?

Who's Your Daddy?

You might recall this scene from *Remember the Titans*, a movie in which Denzel Washington portrays a high school football coach. The coach is approached by one of his players as the team is boarding a bus to go to training camp. The disrespectful young man expresses himself in a manner demeaning to the coach's authority.

"Where're your folks, your parents. Are they here? Where are they?" asks the coach.

The player points at his mother, standing across the parking lot. Washington's character looks at the mother, then back at the son, and says, "Nice. Take a good look at her. Because once you get on that bus, you ain't got no mama no more. You got your buddies on the team and you got your daddy. Now who's your daddy?"

The young man is silent, unsure what to answer.

"Who's your daddy?"

No answer.

"Who's your daddy?" The coach pauses, then demands:

"Who *is* your daddy?"

"You are," the young player finally says.

One of my spiritual daughters was asked the same question, but in a different context. She was learning how to fly a helicopter. The view and the sights were incredible!

"So who's your daddy?" the pilot asked jokingly, sensing her enthusiasm.

"You are!" she answered.

Who's your daddy?

The question is slang for, "Who's in control of things? Who's showing you the ropes? Who's taking care of you?" Sometimes it's meant in a derogatory way, implying control and manipulation and even coercion, and sometimes it's used comically.

The question is a commentary on our times—a generation devoid of the intended intimacy of the family unit—that we compensate through terms reflecting our lack.

> *I believe at the core of every problem we experience as individuals, as generations, and as nations—even in radical Islam—is the issue of connection to a father.*

"For out of the abundance of the heart the mouth speaks."

-Matthew 12:34b

God wants to be the Abba-Father to an entire generation. Abba is Aramaic for "father," a word used to express intimacy and endearment. I don't intend to promote a common, casual, or irreverent depiction of God the Father. He is a Holy God and we honor Him for the glory due His name. Yet even in His holiness, His love is so great He desires us to have the childlike boldness to come to Him as our Daddy, our Papa, in times of need (Hebrews 4:16).

I believe at the core of every problem we experience as individuals, as generations, and as nations – even in radical Islam — is the issue of connection to a father. It's an issue of breech, an issue of broken trust.

I remember when, as a boy, that trust was broken with my own father. My dad was an underwater demolition frogman — today, we would call him a Navy SEAL. We were at the Amphibious Base in Coronado, California. For a young boy to be at the Amphibious Base was bigger than life. Dad had bought me brand new fins and a mask, just like the ones the Navy SEALS used. Dad was already in the water, and I was so excited I could hardly contain myself as I walked up to the edge of the pool. Suddenly, I stopped dead in my tracks as I realized my dad was drunk.

"Jump on in, Doug," he said. "Come on in, son. Jump in."

I wanted so badly to jump, to be with my dad. He could swim like a fish, and I wanted to learn, too. But I was frozen with fear. If he really loved me, why would he be so drunk? Would I be safe with him? Could I trust him?

I couldn't do it — I couldn't jump. I was afraid I would drown because he wasn't in control of his senses. A measure of intimacy with my dad was severed that day and was never restored. And I never learned how to swim.

At some point, we've all experienced broken trust. When it happens repeatedly we unjustly connect our Heavenly Father with our woundedness, hurts, and mistrust resulting from damaged earthly relationships. These roots of pain have resulted in generations of orphans who don't understand the love of a Heavenly Father because they never had the love of an earthly father. They don't know how to trust their Heavenly Father because they were unable to trust their earthly parents.

So now we have a former generation who don't know

how to be good fathers and mothers trying to raise an emerging generation who are also in need. Entire nations have orphaned themselves from the Heavenly Father or have yet to come into the revelation of God as their Father. And churches have forsaken the Father because they have denied the Son. I call it the "de-CHRIST-ing" of our churches.

We are all looking for identity through... affirmation, acceptance, and approval.

We are all looking for identity through what I call the three "A"s: affirmation, acceptance, and approval. We look for it as individuals, as generations and as nations. But the redemptive plan of God is that He *wants* to pour out His grace to this generation, and to entire nations, because He is the Father of all generations and nations!

"But where sin abounded, grace abounded much more," writes Paul (Romans 5:20). So when there is an entire generation "abounding" in the pain of fatherlessness, how much more will God's grace abound to that generation! If the issue is corporate fatherlessness, then the redemptive plan of God is an outpouring of supernatural grace upon a generation that did not receive the love, embrace, or affirmation of earthly fathers.

God is "a father to the fatherless" and a defender of the widow, and sets the "solitary into families" (Psalm 68:5-6, paraphrased). God desires to take orphaned people, dysfunctional in the worldly sense, and set them into the family of the body of Christ.

John the Baptist cried out as a lone voice in the wilderness preparing the way for the coming of the Lord; but the emerging generation is crying out with a corporate voice. It's a cry in the desert: The Lord is coming! The Lord is coming!

Can you hear the cry?

Are you ready to be a part of His multi-generational outpouring of grace?

God is calling forth a generation wandering in the desert of life. He wants to give them a focus of destination and destiny, put a cloak on them like a camel's hair cloak, and empower them to do great things in the name of Christ. He wants to transform a *fatherless* generation into a *prophetic* generation!

God waits with open arms for His prodigals to return, and He has sent His Son to find the lost.

Are we willing to go the extra mile and join Him?

2

Camels in the Wilderness

Camels in the Wilderness

I once was invited to minister at a racial reconciliation meeting in Louisiana, along with another pastor, Levy Knox. During the meeting, Bishop Knox delivered a powerful message he called "The Camels Are Coming," encouraging us, in the context of reconciliation, to accept and serve whatever camels came our way. The message so resonated within me that I soon began to equate it with my ministry to the emerging generation.

Pastor Knox was alluding to the account in Genesis 24, telling of Abraham sending a servant in search of a bride for his son, Isaac. The servant takes ten camels with him on the journey, each bearing not only basic necessities for desert travel, but also gifts for the bride.

"How will I know when I have found the one meant to be Isaac's bride?" the servant asked. As he pondered the question before God, it became clear that the woman would be known by her willingness to serve her master and anyone in need. The servant found such a woman in Rebecca. She was drawing water at the well, but quickly offered to serve him *and* the ten camels who had just journeyed through the desert.

These camels were not only thirsty, they were also dirty, hungry, and smelly. I've been told that one camel could drink up to 40 gallons of water each after completing that desert journey. That means this woman was willing to serve those ten thirsty camels up to 400 gallons of water—and did so! She didn't realize as she served the camels that they were bearing gifts on their backs that she would soon receive. She wasn't looking for the gifts, she simply desired to serve.

Who Are The Camels?

So what does a Bible story about a bride and ten camels have to do with a book about spiritual fathers and a generation of orphans? That's the beauty of God's Word and all the hidden treasures that lie within it!

Abraham is a type of the Heavenly Father, Abraham's servant is a type of the Holy Spirit, and Isaac is a type of Jesus. Today, the Heavenly Father has sent out His Holy Spirit in search of a Bride who is prepared to serve Him and to serve those in need.

And the camels?

We were camels who came out of the wilderness and have now been redeemed. *We* were dirty, smelly, and thirsty, but someone served us. Jesus filled us with His rivers of living water that never run dry, rivers flowing from the throne of God with healing. And He didn't stop there. God quenched our thirsts and began to change our lives.

And the cycle continues as our lives are changed through Christ. As we grow up into Him and represent Him as His Church and Bride, God bids *us* to reach out and rescue others with this same water of life.

When we were dirty and smelly, wounded and bitter, God

fed us and cleaned us up. Many of us lived with addictive behaviors and immoral lifestyles. We searched constantly to cover our pain. We didn't want to feel the hurt, so we kept running and trying anything we could find to satisfy the longing in our soul.

Many in this fatherless generation are the same. They are covering up their fears, insecurities, and pain. Now we – as former camels redeemed by God – have an opportunity to be like Rebecca, the Servant Bride, willing to take on the task at hand regardless of the cost.

The Book of Revelation reveals the Bride preparing herself for Christ, and we are part of that Bride.

> *"...Let us be glad and rejoice and give Him glory, for the marriage of the Lamb has come, and His wife has made herself ready." And to her it was granted to be arrayed in fine linen, clean and bright, for the fine linen is the righteous acts of the saints. Then he said to me, "Write: 'Blessed are those who are called to the marriage supper of the Lamb!'" And he said to me, "These are the true sayings of God."*
>
> *-Revelation 19:7-9*

As we prepare ourselves for the coming of the Lord, we must commit ourselves to a holy life and to seeking God's Kingdom first. We must reach out with the love of God to those who are hungry and thirsty, for as we serve this generation, we are serving our Lord.

Young people today are like those camels coming out of the wilderness, and God is looking for individuals and churches who will serve them and give them a drink.

The Prophetic Mantle

But there is even more to this than the beautiful story of redemption.

John the Baptist came out of the wilderness dressed in camel's hair, wearing a leather belt around his waist and eating locusts and wild honey. He was extreme, radical, passionate, and full of zeal. By wearing the camel hair cloak, he not only comes out of the desert proclaiming the coming of the Lord, but he also represents the camels themselves, the generation emerging from the wilderness.

> *In those days John the Baptist came preaching in the wilderness of Judea, and saying, "Repent, for the kingdom of heaven is at hand!" For this is He who was spoken of by the prophet Isaiah, saying: "The voice of one crying in the wilderness: 'Prepare the way of the Lord; Make His paths straight.'" "And John himself was clothed in camel's hair, with a leather belt around his waist; and his food was locusts and wild honey.*
>
> *-Matthew 3:1-4*

The cloak of camel's hair is symbolic of a prophetic covering. We live in a day in which the church is to go forth in the spirit of John the Baptist, proclaiming the coming of the Lord, liberty to the captives, and healing to the broken-hearted.

The generation emerging from the wilderness are called to be modern-day John the Baptists. Like their predecessor, they are extreme, radical, passionate and full of zeal. God is clothing them in a prophetic mantle, equipping them to do the work He has ordained for them from the very foundations of the world.

As preparation is made for the Lord's return, there will be many in this generation whose hearts will turn back not only to their earthly fathers but to their Heavenly Father as well. God is already pouring out His grace upon this generation who so desperately need Him. Joel 2:28-29 says:

> *"And it shall come to pass afterward that I will pour out My Spirit on all flesh; your sons and your daughters shall*

*prophesy, your old men shall dream dreams, your young
men shall see visions. And also on My menservants and on
My maidservants I will pour out My Spirit in those days."*

God is referring to those who will live an uncompromising
life for Him and boldly proclaim His truth and mercy to spiritually
nomadic people wandering in the wilderness. From this very
generation of wandering drifters will come even more prophets
and prophetesses, who, transformed by the power of God, will
proclaim and prepare the way for the coming of the Lord.

Many of these camels are desperate for change, and they are
looking for someone to guide them. And as they come to know the
living God, they are radical! They aren't ashamed of the Gospel of
Jesus Christ, for it is the power of God unto salvation.

*"For I am not ashamed of the gospel of Christ, for it is the
power of God to salvation for everyone who believes…"*

-Romans 1:16

This generation knows the road of heartache and the pathway
of pain. When they come to Christ, they're ready for sweeping
change. Then from that place of brokenness and gratitude, we see
them going out boldly, proclaiming truth and rescuing others.

3

A Generation in Need

A Generation in Need

In 2002, there were 52 million Americans who had been born between 1922-1945. They are called the "veterans" generation. "Baby boomers" were born between 1945 and 1960, and were followed by "Xers," born between 1960-1980. [1]

"Generation X" is the first to be affected drastically by the lack of fathers. In algebra, X is the unknown quotient. Society gave "Gen Xers" this label, implying they are wandering drifters. *Wikipedia*, an online encyclopedia, says:

> *"Generation X has survived a hurried childhood of divorce, latchkeys, space shuttle explosions, open classrooms, wide-spread public knowledge of political corruption, inflation and recession, post-Vietnam national malaise, environmental disaster, the Islamic Revolution (in Iran), devil-child movies, and a shift from 'G' to 'R' ratings...Divorce became commonplace and affected families of all social and economic backgrounds. Naturally, Gen Xers were affected*

by the continual bombardment of TV images of the nuclear family in contrast to their own; and feelings of inadequacy and isolation from society resulted." [2]

The current generation of young people, known as "The Millennials" or "Generation Y" (those born after 1980) have inherited the fruit of the previous generations, as we can see in these statistics from Ron Luce's website, www.battlecry.com:

- One third has been drunk in the last month, one in four uses illegal drugs, and 8,000 contract a sexually transmitted disease (STD) every day.
- One million "Gen Ys" are pregnant, and 340,000 get abortions every year.
- One in ten has been raped.
- They will see 14,000 sexual references on TV this year, and nine out of ten of them have seen pornography online.
- Half of the "Millennials" are no longer virgins.
- Forty percent have inflicted self-injury.
- One in five has contemplated suicide, and over 1500 of them actually kill themselves every year. [3]

"Gen Ys" are not only fatherless, many of them are angry, confused, and lacking direction. They act like they don't care. They have been hurt and react accordingly. And satan is determined to rob them of their destinies.

From a media blitz that constantly tells them they don't "measure up" to a bombardment of sin meant to desensitize even those who try to fight against it, our young people are faced with immeasurable challenges. Sadly, too many of them face these challenges alone.

When Christians try to preach a Gospel that speaks of a Father God, the younger generation will often respond with cynicism. They have no comprehension of a Heavenly Father because they have no comprehension of an earthly father.

A Crisis of Identity

In my earlier book, *The Fatherless Generation*, I pointed out that 50-60 percent of our young people grow up in single parent homes, and the majority of them don't have a relationship with their father — even if they know who he is. [4]

While teaching at an urban camp of 250 inner city kids, I asked if any had a healthy relationship with their father. The majority of them — tearfully — said they didn't.

At a home for runaway boys and troubled youth where I serve as an advisor, the entry application asks the same question. At one time, of the 620 boys who had been interviewed, less than 20 of them claimed to have a healthy relationship with their father.

Pastor Jack Graham from PowerPoint Ministries quotes on his "Father Knows Best" CD album that the average American father spends eight minutes a day with his children. [5] According to the Generation Xcel newsletter, 24 million children in the United States live with "absent fathers," and 20 million live in single parent homes. The newsletter also quotes statistics from The National Fatherhood Initiative which indicate that 40 percent of children in father-absent homes have not even seen their dads within the past year. Fifty percent have never set foot in their father's home, and 26 percent of absent fathers don't even live in the same state as their children. [6]

How sad for a nation that once took pride not only in knowing the Heavenly Father but was also known for the strength of its families, especially its fathers.

Many fathers today are in an identity crisis. This results in women with an identity crisis, trying to be father and mother, nurturer and disciplinarian. That leads to children growing up with an identity crisis, confused about genders and roles within their own families because they have no role models to follow.

The book *Rachel's Tears* chronicles the life of Rachel Scott, one of the students who died for her faith in the Columbine High School shootings in 1999. Much of the book is taken from her own journal writings as well as observations from her parents. Rachel's father and mother separated when she was seven years old and later divorced.

After her tragic and premature death, Rachel's parents discovered through her journal entries how she had felt torn between her parents with conflicting loyalties and feelings of abandonment. Their daughter's pain came as a surprise because her faith in God and bold witness were so strong. They knew the divorce would be hard on their children, so her parents wisely committed to never speak ill of one another. They loved their daughter immensely and did everything they could to ease the pain, but it was still a struggle. Even her father, Darrell Scott, says, "Regardless of the reasons for a divorce it is never easy when children are involved. Children will always be affected by divorce."[7]

Our Heavenly Father revealed His perfect plan at the dawn of creation, which was, and still is, one man and one woman, together raising a family. He never intended for a child to pick between a mom and dad. He never intended for the woman to be both nurturer and disciplinarian. He never intended for men to go through the identity crisis they are going through now and to be emasculated by the "Jezebel spirit" so prevalent in our day, undermining them in the roles God has given them. The spiritual, mental and emotional entropy pulling at men, women, and children today was not His design.

So what do we do as a church in the context of this reality? How do we get back to a place where the Lord is the nucleus of our families, our generations, and our nation?

We must turn our focus back to God the *Father*.

In the Garden of Eden, God placed the *Tree of Life* in the center of the garden. But when satan tempted Eve, her focus had shifted. Her discourse with him shows that the *Tree of Good and Evil* had become, in her mind, the center of the garden. Her focus had shifted — from all that God had given to her — to the one thing she lacked.

God desires to bring strength back to men so they can guide, guard, and govern their homes with the love of Christ. When this happens, security will return to the home for the mothers and the children. But God's *greatest* desire is to be our Father and to bring us into His family through the Spirit of Adoption.

A Generation Lost

Throughout history, satan's plan has been to kill destinies while they are yet in their infancy. Pharaoh slew the infants in Egypt trying to kill Moses. Herod murdered the male infants in the hope of killing Jesus. Now, satan is targeting our youth and children at their most vulnerable ages to keep them from entering their God-ordained destinies.

Satan knows this generation is set apart by God for mighty exploits, in spite of the grim statistics and what looks hopeless to the natural eye. The destroyer knows his time is short, and he is doing everything possible to postpone the inevitable and distract this generation from fulfilling its true destiny in Christ Jesus.

From September of 2000 through November of 2003, I had the pleasure of serving with "The Call." During this series of youth gatherings, birthed from the vision of Lou Engle and Che Ahn, we saw the body of Christ come together in multi-generational gatherings to empower the emerging generation. More than one million young people gathered in seven locations across America, beginning in Washington D.C. and ending at the Cotton Bowl in Dallas, along with various international venues. Each event consisted of an entire day of prayer, fasting and worship — from sun-up to sundown. There were no performances, no personal agendas. There was only a multi-generational outcry in praise, worship, and passionate prayers for God to touch the emerging generation.

The reason we chose Dallas for "The Call Texas" was because we believed Dallas played a major role in birthing the "death culture." It was in Dallas where abortion was made legal in 1973 with the passing of Roe vs. Wade, unleashing a travesty of death across the nation. Since that time, almost 50 million lives have been taken before taking their first breath.

Do you comprehend the significance of that number, the stark reality of it all? Over 50 million lives! No matter what a person believes about abortion, it is absolutely tragic that *an entire generation* of lives has been sacrificed on the altar of irresponsibility and convenience in this modern-day holocaust that is readily accepted and even defended by our society and blessed by our lawmakers. Revelation 21: 4 says:

> *"…God will wipe away every tear from their eyes; there shall be no more death, nor sorrow, nor crying. There shall be no more pain, for the former things have passed away."*

At "The Call Dallas," I spoke this Scripture over these generations, declaring: "No more death! It's time to take off the grave clothes! It's time to take off the things that are binding us and hindering us from walking in the fullness of all that He has for us. It's time to come forth!"

Kids Who Care

Tim Clinton, president of the American Association of Christian Counselors, wrote in one of his letters to AACC members: "In a nation that claims to be very dedicated to kids, shamefully they are our most under-served population. And with the exception of the adults who care about children, they have no advocate." He goes on to quote Fran Stott, who said, "Every child needs at least one person who is crazy about them."[8]

The enemy wants our children to believe there is no one who cares about them. He wants us all to believe an unborn life is not a life at all. But even as he ruthlessly attacks, God's Spirit is moving just as mightily among children in many areas throughout the world.

George and Pam, our missionaries to Southeast Asia, began a children's prayer initiative in one of the country's where they served. Now, the ministry is actually led by a young woman who learned how to pray through her involvement with the ministry, and who took over the leadership at age 15. Others we know have shared reports of children in India, Indonesia, and other locations who are moving in prophetic and healing gifts.

We also see God raising up children who are expressing His heart through their compassion for the hurting. We call them "Kids Who Care."

Katia and her family are originally from Iran, but are now my Houston neighbors. They are also brothers and sisters in the Lord. One Christmas, things were tough for the family, and the father was working two jobs. One was part-time at a local fast food restaurant where I stop for my morning coffee. We were in the middle of our Holiday of Hope program, collecting food and toys and distributing funds to thousands of families throughout the city. After visiting Katia's father one day, I decided I wanted to do something special for the family during the holidays.

Meanwhile, unbeknownst to me, God had touched Katia's heart to help Somebody Cares with our ministry to the children of the city at Christmas. She set up a table at her church one Sunday to sell her own hand-drawn pictures. Before her family received any kind of gift from Somebody Cares, she came to my house to present a small ceramic Christmas container filled with coins as a donation to the work of our ministry.

I was overwhelmed by this little girl's ability to see past her own needs and to have compassion for others. I thought of the story of David when his mighty men broke through the armies of the Philistines to bring him a drink from the well of Bethlehem. Like David, I felt unworthy to receive this precious gift. It still sits on my bookshelf as a reminder to me of this one child's heart of compassion and generosity.

K.J. is another one of our "Kids Who Care." He was five years old when he saw news stories about families who lost everything in Hurricane Katrina. Immediately he began packing up his own toys to send to them. This small act of compassion led to a campaign throughout the city of Omaha that resulted in a truckload of toys arriving at our offices in Houston, which were then distributed to hurricane evacuees during Christmas. He and his mother even flew here to help give them away.

Alyson had heard about our ministry to hurricane evacuees because of our connection with the church where her father is a pastor in York, Pennsylvania. On her tenth birthday, she asked her friends not to bring gifts to her party but to bring money for hurricane relief instead. They sent us $220.

Amanda was also 10 when she visited New Orleans with her parents during a Somebody Cares hurricane relief outreach. She was so moved at the immense loss and destruction caused by Hurricane Katrina, she went throughout her neighborhood painting faces to raise money for the children in New Orleans.

A Wake-Up Call

We called the last "Call" event "The Wake-Up Call," recognizing that if we neglect this great responsibility to become fathers to this generation, we will lose them to the wiles of the enemy.

The late Fuchsia Picket, when speaking at Rock City Church in Baltimore, delivered a message about the great move of the *Holy Spirit* from the early 1900s, bringing about a great restoration of the Spirit's work within churches everywhere. Then, in the 1960s and 1970s, the *Jesus Movement* emerged.

Because the Trinity includes three Persons, she said, the next great move throughout the land would be one focusing on *the father heart of God*, beginning when the hearts of the fathers turn to the children and the hearts of the children turn to the fathers (See Malachi 4:6). Significantly, the first of "The Call" rallies focused on this theme to begin the revolutionary release of the father heart of God not only within the church, but through whole communities. More than 425,000 people attended this first rally, held on The Mall in Washington, D.C. in September 2000.

As I've participated in movements like "The Call," "Joshua Generation," "Chain Reaction," and others, I've realized there is a ground-swell from this wandering generation calling out, "We want to connect to something." They are not satisfied with the *status quo*, but are crying out to God: "We want the blessing of the Father! We want the covering of our parents and our spiritual parents! We want to be released into our uniqueness!"

The present generation is looking for the embrace and the affirmation of a father. And when they come into the revelation of their Heavenly Father, there's a radical response. They're willing to do whatever it takes to be that prophetic generation.

God has been giving wake-up calls to us all. We've experienced the challenges around the world, the global uncertainties and shiftings, the increase in natural disasters, the wars and rumors of wars. Yet, in the midst of it all, God is raising up a multi-generational army to honor Him, honor one another, and release this emerging generation to its destiny.

It's been a wake-up call, and many of us have been pushing our snooze buttons. But now it's time. There is a clarion call from God for this generation to rise up and fulfill the words spoken over it in Scripture.

Could it be that, in this genera-tion, we will see the culmination of all the words spoken by the prophets of old? Is it possible this generation is coming into its destiny to prepare the way for the coming of the Lord?

A Prophetic Culmination

The former generations are crucial to this plan because God is calling us to parent, guide, bless, and release them to do mighty exploits for Him.

Statistics paint a grim picture of a future that seems almost hopeless. Nonetheless, God is still in charge, and many from this emerging generation have already come forth despite the barrage of attacks coming against them. And when they do, they are full of zeal and a passionate desire to do great things for the Lord.

God wants to take the misfit Generation X and make it into Generation Excellent, a Generation of Expectancy for the coming revival. He wants to take Generation Y and use them to lead His people into the Promised Land.

But they are not *just* the Joshuas, John the Baptists, Elishas, or Elijahs. They constitute the *prophetic generation* because God is taking the culmination of all those anointings and exponentially bringing them together for this season!

The former generations are crucial to this plan because God is calling us to parent, guide, bless, and release them to do mighty exploits for Him. If the Bride does not do her part in obeying Christ's mandate to come alongside and empower the young, the devil will continue to destroy the very ones God wants to raise up. He will continue the onslaught of abortions, gangs, kids killing kids and suicide.

Satan is trying to rob identities and destinies, but this generation is not lost. It needs direction to find its way out of the wilderness, and we who have gone before are the ones who can show them.

Will we be like Rachel, who wept over the bloodshed of a generation? Or will we be like Elizabeth, who rejoiced over the release of her generation's forerunner? The responsibility is up to us. May God's purpose prevail!

4

A Nation of Orphans

A Nation of Orphans

There is an identity crisis in America, but it is not limited to the emerging generation.

Our society is one in which liberal educators are rewriting textbooks and denying even the Founding Fathers. We are fatherless and orphaned in a historical sense, a spiritual sense, and a practical sense.

We are witnessing the "de-CHRIST-ing" of our nation. The only One who is pure of heart and pure of purpose, who is liberator and justice giver, is Jesus Christ. When we take Him out of the equation, there is no liberty, salvation, deliverance, or healing because these do not exist on earth without the name of Jesus. To take away the spiritual and moral values from a people is to leave them with nothing but the journey to anarchy, because to deny the Son is also to deny the Father.

> *To take away the spiritual and moral values from a people is to leave them with nothing but the journey to anarchy.*

Many people have denied almost any authority, especially God's authority. Those who stand for righteousness are mocked. It seems as if America is shouting, "We don't want God!" — except, of course, when we want His blessings. This is much like a teenager who has nothing do with his parents and denies their authority until he wants the keys to the car.

We want God on our terms, not His. He becomes whoever or whatever we want Him to be. We forget God created us in His own image, so we try to re-create Him in our own image.

Just as children without a father's teaching and discipline follow a path of rebellion and lawlessness, so does a nation whose people neglect their responsibilities to be what God has preordained. Without the direction and discipline of our Heavenly Father in society, we will continue to see a rise in violence, immorality, and lawlessness in our communities. These are realities we must face. They are the inevitable consequences of fatherlessness.

God ordained America to be a nation that would honor Him, but we have turned our backs on Him. We have not only orphaned ourselves from God the Heavenly Father, but from our Founding Fathers. In effect, we are denying the One for whom they gave their lives and upon whose principles they established the laws of the land. And we are now reaping the results.

Blessed is the nation whose God is the Lord.

-Psalm 33: 12a

Faulty Foundations

My friend Curt from Youth-Reach Houston was in the Gulf Coast area immediately after Hurricane Ivan hit in 2004. He saw the destruction and devastation left in Ivan's path—not only shattered dwellings, but also broken lives and dreams. I experienced the same thing when I visited New Orleans and the Gulf Coast areas of Mississippi after the tragic destruction of Hurricane Katrina in 2005.

Just as houses built on the sands of our beaches could not withstand Ivan or Katrina, neither will we withstand the shaking that is coming. As long as our nation sits on a cracked and unstable foundation, we will not be able to survive the storms of life.

That is where America is today. Just as a family without a father is shaky, vulnerable, and out of balance, so too are we as a nation. We are like a house built on sand, with a cracked and very faulty foundation. And though it may appear to the outside world and even to ourselves that our foundation is intact, when the storms of life come — be it economic, spiritual, or natural disasters — our house is going to crumble.

A Vision of Hope

Prior to a Presidential election, I was invited to deliver the invocation at one of the largest state gatherings of any political party. There were more than 17,000 people in attendance. The Lord put it on my heart to present the need for a revival of character from the pulpits all the way to the White House.

I stated how a great leader named Solomon said, *"Hope deferred makes the heart sick"* (Proverbs 13:12). Then I quoted the great King Hezekiah, who once said, in a day of trouble and distress, *"The children are ready to come to birth, but there is no strength to deliver them."* (2 Kings 19:3).

We live, I said, in the same kind of predicament. We have a whole generation of young people either sacrificed before they are born or being brought to birth but left with no vision of hope or purpose.

We need to give such a vision again – a vision of hope, a vision of purpose, a vision of destination. We cannot do this through institutional Christianity, shallow platitudes, or business as usual. We can only cast vision by returning to Jesus as our first love, being lovesick for His presence, and once again embracing our Heavenly Father as Lord of our hearts and Lord over our land.

Human wisdom and man-made efforts have failed us. As Scripture tells us, *"Unless the LORD builds a house, they labor in vain who build it."* (Psalm 127:1)

What's In It For Me?

Drugs, alcohol, and gangs are not the real problem. They are by-products of a deeper dilemma. Drugs and alcohol provide escape from a world of pain. Gangs provide a sense of "family" to those who have none. External expressions of rebellion are outward signs of internal hurt.

> *We need to give such a vision again – a vision of hope, a vision of purpose, a vision of destination.*

I attribute many of the problems in America to my own generation—the "baby boomers," those of us born post-World War II and into the early 1960s. I was on the tail end of of the "boomer" generation. Our mindset, which affected our children, caused us to be characterized as the "me-generation." Our motto was, "if it feels good, do it." Our ethical philosophy was embodied in the statement, "I'm not hurting anybody else; it's my life and I'll do what I want." Character was irrelevant. Commitment was unnecessary.

This lack of character and commitment produced legalized abortion, higher divorce rates, and single-parent homes where women are both mother and father to their children. Men abdicated their influence by not taking responsibility for their actions and not being Christlike in their behavior toward women, and women responded with the feminist movement.

What should have been an era of godly liberation and spiritual freedom led to a national identity crisis. Without proper release, what should have brought freedom brought more bondage. Engaging in relationship without commitment led to a chasm not only between genders but birthed the gap between the generations as well.

Unfortunately, this "me" culture even permeated the atmosphere of some our churches, often producing Christians who ask themselves, "What make me feel good?" Yes, we need to be relevant, but if our teaching does not get past the surface, those we disciple will have nothing to stand on when they are hit by the storms of life.

Like the Shulamite in Song of Songs, we must be lovesick once again for God. "Revival comes by desperation," said Jackson Senyonga of Uganda, "and desperation comes one of two ways: passion or persecution." The late Leonard Ravenhill understood the same principle. "God doesn't answer prayer," he said, "He answers desperate prayer." And I would add to that, "God answers desperate and *passionate* prayer."[1]

Our passion for God allows no room for mediocrity or compromise. God is not looking for shallow platitudes or religious incantations. Nor does He desire a surface relationship in which His children interact with Him only when they want something. God desires intimacy and conversation with His creation.

> *Our passion for God allows no room for mediocrity or compromise.*

God our Father does not want to be seen as a "sugar daddy" in the sky. He wants relationship with His children. Just as a child needs affirmation from his father, so does a father need to be honored and respected by his children. Blessings flow as the result of this intimate engagement. Don't seek the blessing, but seek the Father.

Muddy Religion

We live in a nation of muddy religion—a place where New Age philosophy mingles with Buddhism; where Atheism,

Hinduism, self-awareness, and Christianity are all tossed together in a "religion stew." It is no wonder our youth have little concept of absolute truth. "Nationwide, there are now more Buddhists than Presbyterians and nearly as many Muslims as Jews."[2]

"...Many Americans seek spiritual sustenance beyond organized religion, in personal experiences and meditative practices. More than 4 out of 5 Americans say they have 'experienced God's presence or a spiritual force' close to them, and 46 percent say it has happened many times. 'People are reaching out in all directions in their attempt to escape from the seen world to the unseen world,' explains pollster George Gallup Jr. 'There is a deep desire for spiritual moorings — a hunger for God.'"[3]

The bottom line is this: the hunger is there. The world is searching for what popular culture terms "spirituality." People will continue to find it in alternative ways if we do not point the way to the One True Answer.

A Matter of Family

God is unleashing a multi-generational anointing, but the enemy is unleashing a multi-generational attack. It's not only an assault on the biological family, but also upon the spiritual family — the church — and it's a battle we must fight first and foremost on our knees. It's a battle we fight by drawing closer in intimacy to the One who gives us liberty and life.

We cannot take lightly our responsibilities to be a beacon of truth to the upcoming generations and to the world. My spiritual father Ed Cole used to say, "You cannot compensate through sacrifice what you lose through disobedience."

Those who live outside our borders will tell us that if the church in America ever falls, so will the lives and liberties of those who dwell in other nations across the globe. Our very futures hang in the balance, as do the destinies of our families, our nation, and the emerging generation. Our churches are sick and orphaned because they have forsaken their Father. They have left their first love.

But Jesus Christ remains our Savior, Healer, Deliverer, and Liberator. There is nothing too difficult for Him if He is truly on the thrones of our hearts and on the thrones of the pulpits in America.

The curses of past generations are broken when we allow God to work through our churches to change the present generation. We can't fix things in our own strength, but if we make ourselves available, God can use us to reach the generations for Him. He can heal us and seal us, through the Spirit of Adoption, so we can be fathers and mothers to those coming after us.

God is challenging us to live a life of excellence and to do all that we do unto Him—serving one another, the body of Christ, and the lost. If we do this, the world, our nation, and the emerging generation will see the love of the body of Christ and be drawn to the Father because they have a hunger for genuine truth. People must see something different about us so that they can be drawn to our genuineness. Matthew 5:16 says:

> *"Let your light so shine before men, that they may see your good works and glorify your Father in heaven."*

God wants us to take off our lampshades so His light and life can shine through us and draw all men—from all nations and all generations—unto Him.

Part II

Where Do Daddies Come From?

5

Leading by Example

Leading by Example

"Mommy, where do daddies come from?" asked a child in a Jim Borgman cartoon *(Cincinnati Enquirer, 1994)*.

In some cases that hard question has supplanted the awkward query, *Where do babies come from?* Mothers are sometimes stumped in their efforts to explain the absence of a father in a child's life. Instead of the cornerstone of the family, a father has become a commodity.

How can we—from a generation where so many of us grew up without understanding the love of earthly mothers and fathers—be spiritual mothers and fathers to others?

How can we help this emerging generation understand the love of a Heavenly Father?

In 1981, we began our ministry by reaching out to the lost on the streets of Houston. Though the life experiences of the youth we encountered were different, they almost always had one thing in common—the absence of a father.

Today, ministries such as Montrose Street Reach, part of our Somebody Cares Houston network of ministries, continues the work we began in the 1980s. At one of their annual fundraising banquets, street kids who had come to know Jesus shared their testimonies. The common denominator in their pathways to destruction—from which God has rescued them—was physical, sexual, or emotional abuse, sometimes coming directly from their father himself or coming indirectly from the lack of a father's presence and protection in the home.

> *We have a responsibility to a generation— statistically proven to be fatherless— looking for spiritual fathers.*

We have a responsibility to a generation—statistically proven to be fatherless—looking for spiritual fathers. We must adopt this orphaned generation and direct them toward our Heavenly Father, who desires to seal them all with His Spirit of Adoption.

At the same time, many in my generation don't know how to be good fathers—including me. But those who are desperate for fathers are not expecting us to know *how*, but to be *willing*. Willingness brings a release of God's grace to enable us.

Learning to Lead

In the spring of 2004, I hosted a "think tank" for "emerging leaders of the emerging generation." What started as a small gathering escalated into an attendance of more than 60 leaders from across the country, including youth workers and college ministry leaders, worship leaders, seasoned pastors, marketplace ministers, ministry networkers, intercessors, and others. As each of them spoke, the recurring theme was the need for spiritual fathers.

I already knew our younger generation was looking for spiritual fathers. That's why I invited those who are serving on the front lines in "out of the box" ministries. What surprised me, however, was the need these *leaders* expressed for spiritual fathers!

When those of us who were older responded and said we don't know how to be good fathers because we were fatherless, too, they said, "We're not asking you to know how. And we're not asking you to be perfect. We're not even asking you to give us anything. But would you journey with us? We want to know there's someone who has gone before us, someone who can be there for us, just to give us advice. We want to know we can call you. We want to know you're praying for us. We don't need a lot of time. We just need to know we can connect."

Just like the generation they are leading, the leaders are looking for connection and covering.

One young minister ordained by our organization who considers me a spiritual father said, "I got saved, was raised in church, backslid, recommitted, and struggled for many years because I didn't have a spiritual father." As a result, his ministry is now centered on spiritual fathering. "If it isn't relational," he said, "we don't do it."

Pastor Mike of Freedom International Church in Houston shared insights about "the marks of a father," which he relates to fathers in the spiritual as well as the natural.

"A spiritual father," he said, "knows how to discipline his children with mercy, grace, and love." In I Samuel 4, Eli does not correct his sons, even though they are involved in immorality and are not following God's commands regarding sacrifices and offerings. The result is the downfall of Eli's ministry. On his watch, Pastor Mike reminds us, the Ark of the Lord — which represents the presence of God — was stolen from the temple. In that same regard, a spiritual father is able to discern his true sons and daughters, those who are faithful, those who won't leave when they are disciplined, those who will protect the DNA and reputation of the ministry.

Mike also quotes the apostle Paul when he talks about the importance of a father's travailing prayers for his children:

My dear children, for whom I am again in the pains of childbirth until Christ is formed in you…

-Galatians 4:19 (NIV)

"Some things will only come to pass," Mike says, "if a father is pressing in through the pain of travailing, the pain of prayer, and the pain of fasting. Lots of spiritual fathers complain about their children or the staff God has sent to them. As fathers, they know the destinies of those children. But they do not always go to war for that destiny."

Rusty, a pastor in Sealy, Texas, puts it this way: "Many times, there is a treasure inside a youth's heart but they don't recognize it so they run after the treasure in someone else's heart. A spiritual father has to help them see the treasure in their own hearts."

I remember when Ruben began coming to the ministry and was insecure about his reading ability. I encouraged him to get his GED, and now he preaches and teaches the Bible at our weekly worship service when I'm away. I saw how Kathy had a gift for counseling, so I encouraged her to get training. God uses her gift daily as she ministers to people who call or come to our office for help with material, emotional, and physical needs.

Curt, from Youth-Reach Houston, shares another real-life illustration of coming alongside in a practical way:

"During one of the many projects we do at Youth-Reach, I was in need of a specific tool to complete the job. I looked over at one of the boys, a resident of only a month or so who had likely never held a tool in his life, and asked him to get me a crescent wrench from our workshop. He said OK and took off to get it for me. A few minutes later he returned. Without saying a word he held out to me a set

of channel locks — which is a large pair of adjustable pliers — not a crescent wrench. I could see in his eyes that he had looked at all the tools on the wall in the workshop and just guessed that this was what I was asking for. It was also clear that he was really hoping he had guessed right. He wanted to please me, and he had tried his best.

You see, many of our boys arrive in baggy clothes with a gang affiliation and a long arrest record. They appear tough, but plain old hard work exposes that they are weak, soft, and without the basic knowledge of how to really be a man.

I left the project behind and that boy and I went to the workshop. Without embarrassing him, we went over all the tools hanging there on the wall. He drank it all in and asked questions whenever he did not grasp the use of each tool. It was so clear at that moment something was missing — or more specifically, SOMEONE was missing. His father should have been doing this, but it was not to be. That man had abandoned his little boy. It was my personal joy to step into his role of daddy for just a few minutes.

I have had the honor of doing that with hundreds of abandoned boys. It is important to teach young men the Word of God. It is also important to teach them how to hold a hammer, how to speak to girls, and how to keep a checkbook. These are simple life lessons, but

"We are experiencing the fallout of a nation that has found it acceptable to procreate at will then abandon their offspring."

without a father, who will teach them?

We are experiencing the fallout of a nation that has found it acceptable to procreate at will then abandon their offspring. This generation of boys is looking for a daddy, and if we, the church, can look beyond our programs and our buildings, we will find a generation of world-changers right outside our doors. But do we really care to pay the emotional, spiritual and financial cost that will be demanded to reclaim them? The answer to that question is yet to be heard."

My Greatest Joy

One of my greatest joys is to hear members of the younger generation tell me they feel empowered when I come to visit them in their ministries.

They feel valued and validated by a spiritual father. God has taken me, someone who has no idea how to be a father in the natural, and used me to spiritually father many.

I led Randy to the Lord in 1981, and he proudly calls himself "the first Turning Pointer" after the name of our parent ministry, Turning Point Ministries International, which began as a Bible study in my workout studio. Randy was a professional dancer at the time and had been the Texas disco champion. Now he leads "Dance Ad Deum," a troupe that tours the world and dances for the glory of God.

Once when I returned from an international trip, I had a Father's Day message on my voice mail Randy had left for me while I was away. "This is your son, Randall. I just wanted to thank you for being such a good father and friend. You raised me well."

Michael also calls me every Father's Day. One year, he left a beautiful letter for me at the office, thanking me for being a spiritual father, not even knowing how much at that moment I needed the encouragement.

J.T. is another spiritual son from the early days of the ministry. His father had been shot and killed years earlier, and the anger and the pain held him hostage to thoughts of revenge. But after J.T. received the Spirit of Adoption through the salvation of Christ and came to know his Heavenly Father, he was able to forgive and walk in that forgiveness. Today, he is a successful businessman, husband, and father, and he serves on our Board of Directors. His daughter calls me "Uncle Dougie."

Russ was addicted to drugs as a young man, and his family contacted me when they had nowhere else to turn. I was able to minister to him and help him get into a program. "Thanks to you," he wrote to me once, "my kids never had to see their dad drunk or on drugs. You are an example to me of what I aspire to be."

Dale was a part of our ministry for many years before moving back to Pittsburgh. In 2004, I had the privilege of reading Scriptures in his wedding. He was 53 and marrying for the first time. During the weekend's festivities, I was honored when he publicly shared that he had two spiritual fathers: one was the late John Osteen, and the other was me.

Monica now serves at a nearby church pastored by one of my friends. Although I could not be there when they ordained her for ministry, I wrote a letter that was read during the ceremony, giving her a father's blessing and letting her know how proud of her I am. She told me later the letter brought tears to her eyes. When she was graduating with her Master's degree, she wanted her "daddy" to come to that celebration as well.

Kathy never knew her biological father, and her mother died when she was young. She came to our ministry in 1996 during Prayer Mountain, a city-wide gathering of prayer, worship, and fasting which we hosted the last 40 days of 1996. Obeying God's prompting, she began volunteering for us, then later came on staff. When she was going through a season of personal difficulties and was abandoned by her husband, God allowed me to be a spiritual father to her by insuring she was taken care of financially through her employment with the ministry. Kathy ministers now to the singles at her church and has her own ministry to widows. She never misses an opportunity to honor me as one of her fathers.

Cindy was a teen-ager struggling with rejection and thoughts of suicide. The Lord led her to a Catholic church where we presented the Gospel through one of our dramas, and she gave her life to Jesus that night. Now, she has three beautiful daughters who come with her when she volunteers in the office, and her husband is active in our men's ministry.

The list goes on: Ruben, Cynthia, Tim, Mike, Michael, Lance, Kevin, Jeremy, Jamie, Laura, Andrew, John, Debbie, Marti, Bob, Scott . . . so many people who acknowledge me as one of their spiritual fathers.

In *The Fatherless Generation*, I quoted a definition for "father" from Dr. Ed Cole. He said a father is the one who guides, guards, and governs in the home. He is the one who brings proper discipline, strength, and direction to the family unit.[1]

This is the biblical definition of fatherhood, and it's a model we can use to be spiritual fathers to our spiritual families, as well.

Leading By Example

This fatherless, orphaned generation needs those who will show them the love of their Heavenly Father. Without proper, godly role models in the home, young people are left to find their own way through life's journey.

Leading by example is a major component of God's plan for older generations. Something is desperately wrong when one generation is unable to successfully transmit its values to its children and grandchildren. The scriptural norm is found in Psalm 145:4:

"One generation will commend your works to another; they will tell of your mighty acts. They will speak of the glorious splendor of your majesty." NIV

God wants us to be the kind of leaders who inspire younger generations to commend our works through Him. God wants one of our top priorities to be sharing the Gospel and power of God with those for whom we are fathers and mothers, spiritually as well as biologically.

But even many families that are intact are finding it difficult to convince their children to follow their values. In fact, researchers with the National Study of Youth and Religion concluded "American teens believe in a combination of works-based righteous-ness, religion as psychological well-being, and a distant, non-interfering god."[2] How could this be? Why do so many Christian parents struggle to raise children who are radically committed to Christ?

How could this be? The answer is sad to admit: Many of us have lived a lukewarm, uninspiring Christian life unappealing to our children. They see our compromise and conclude that they don't want what we have. Again, who can blame them?

Hypocritical Christianity isn't very attractive.

The writer of Hebrews tells us we have those in the great "Hall of Faith" watching us from the grandstands as "a great cloud of witnesses."

And all these, having obtained a good testimony through faith, did not receive the promise, God having provided something better for us, that they should not be made perfect apart from us. Therefore we also, since we are surrounded by so great a cloud of witnesses, let us lay aside every weight, and the sin which so easily ensnares us, and let us run with endurance the race that is set before us...

-Hebrews 11:39-12:1

Isn't it amazing that only "together with us" will the great heroes of faith be made perfect? In the same way, our own destinies are inextricably tied to both those who have preceded us and those who will follow us in the relay race of life. Because of this fact, no task is more important than successfully passing our faith to the next generation.

Leonard Ravenhill once told our staff:

The spiritual battle for the moral soul of a generation should provoke us to put our priorities in perspective, bringing to light the biblical mandate of every believer to be a tangible expression of Christ.

"Starting with only 120 people in the upper room, the early Christians had no Bibles, concordances, seminaries, church buildings or modern media, but they had an enduement of power from on high. With scarcely any human resources, they turned the world upside down. Today, in contrast, we have more than 120 million believers who claim to be filled with the Holy Spirit—yet we have generally failed to turn the world upside down. We have all the resources, money and Bible colleges, yet we lack a genuine enduement of spiritual power."

We have a nation full of concordances and Bibles that collect dust, but God invests His anointing in men and women of character so they can affect and infect a whole generation. Revival of character and God's anointing come with many purposes, including redeeming young people who have been spiritually aborted and abandoned by a self-centered society and a church that is often apathetic. The spiritual battle for the moral soul of a generation should provoke us to put our priorities in perspective, bringing to light the biblical mandate of every believer to be a tangible expression of Christ.

The Kingdom of God is built on relationships. As followers of Christ, the proof of our love is reflected by the kindness and compassion we show others. Yet, far too often we are so engulfed in our personal challenges that we neglect the very things that attract God's favor and blessings.

We live in such an impersonal, systems-structured society that, rather than people imitating us as we imitate Christ, they are left to become clones of nothing more than modern-day institutional Christianity. They are "programmed" through our structures and activities in churches that are often much too similar to the world they left behind.

The present young generation needs to see that we are who we say we are. They need to see us walk our talk. They need to see that we are the same people at home that we are at church. They need to see we are different from the world.

As we respond to our struggles by displaying the fruits of the character of God — and not in bitterness and anger — our walk will begin to speak, inspire, and direct. It will begin to bring vision and hope to a generation that hungers for substance.

The Desire for Connection

I gained some insight recently into how we pass along that vision and hope. The insight came regarding the biblical practice of "laying on of hands." Even though hands were laid on people to impart healing and ordain them to ministry, one of the original roots of the practice was to pass on "the blessing" from one generation to another, like Jacob did with his sons.

Laying on of hands is not something you can do by phone, e-mail, or fax. You have to *be there*. One of the tragedies for many young people is that they don't have parents who are truly *there* for them, in person and by example. They don't have dads and moms present in person to impart to them the value or even the techniques of interaction.

They are however, very skilled with technology! These young people can find their way around the latest electronic devices with ease — computers, chat rooms, I-pods, text messages. However, this comes often at the cost of personal intimacy.

Contrast this to my generation, who grew up with board games and athletic activities as our recreation. We relied on personal visits, telephones, even writing letters to keep in touch. Our communities were built around churches and schools. Whether we had model parents or absentee fathers, we at least knew our neighbors. Our relationships were personal. And when our country was founded, entire communities were centered around the church and the water well – the two places of "life."

A staff associate told the story of three young brothers sitting on a couch, each playing their own Game Boys. They were in the same room, side by side on the sofa, yet there was no interaction, no conversation, no communication. We see it on a larger scale in other venues as well: internet cafes and coffee shops filled with young people working on their own laptops, not necessarily interacting with each other but obviously feeling the need to be connected through a social setting.

Then there's the popularity of internet sites like "myspace," where kids can connect with each other via cyberspace.

"The danger today is that young people can have relationships without any personal interaction."

"I've seen 'myspace' sites where kids have 5000 'friends,'" says my friend Mike. "There are people in every generation who are very relational and people in every generation who are very withdrawn. The danger today is that young people can have relationships without any personal interaction."

In their hearts, Mike says, they are crying out to be a part of something, longing to be connected. They just don't always know how to do it. Even the fact that they frequent coffeehouses and cyber cafés confirms an innate desire to be connected to a bigger picture.

The Personal Touch

I prefer the personal touch. I don't like voice mail or automated prompts. But we live in such an impersonal society, even in our churches. We need to get back to the personal touch because God is a personal God.

An Australian television commercial depicts a young Japanese couple in the delivery room celebrating the arrival of their newborn baby. "How cute! How cute!" say the doctors and nurses to the proud parents. As the camera moves in to show us the sweet face of the little one wrapped snuggly in his blanket, the newborn suddenly whips out a Fuji camera and takes a picture of his surprised and astonished parents! The inferred message, of course, is that all Japanese are born with a camera in their hands!

When it comes to technology, we need the knowledge, skill, and finesse of the younger generation; but in turn, we can impart to them this gift of personal touch and the value of face-to-face interaction.

Although I was born in Japan and my mother was Japanese, I'm not exactly the typical Asian stereotype. In fact, I didn't even own a digital camera until I was given one for my 48th birthday by a church whose pastor wants me to get back to my Asian roots.

You could probably say, instead, that I was born with a phone in my ear instead of a camera in my hands. People say I'm always on the phone, and that's because I love to keep in touch with people. And no matter what time of day or night I happen to be awake, there is someone in the world I can call on the phone—

whether they're in Malaysia, Africa, Fiji, Australia, or some other part of the U.S. — just to let them know I am thinking about them.

When it comes to technology, we need the knowledge, skill, and finesse of the younger generation; but in turn, we can impart to them this gift of personal touch and the value of face-to-face interaction.

Matt, an emerging generational leader, told me how he demonstrated the love of God in this way to his oldest son, Joshua, who was 12 at the time. Josh is strong and muscular and growing up very much in the image of his dad.

Matt and his wife, Katy, coordinate a youth initiative throughout the Northeast including Baltimore, New York City, and various locations in New England. One day, during an outreach in Lowell, Massachusetts, the teams of young people were in an intense time of prayer and worship. They had been out all day serving the community with work projects.

Just a year earlier, I had been the keynote speaker for their outreach in that same community. Several of the interns ministered to me during a time of prayer led by Matt and Katy's 10-year-old son Caleb, who had been a pivotal part of the outreach with his energy, zeal, and enthusiasm. Just a few days after I left, Caleb went to be with Jesus as the result of a car accident.

Josh was also in the accident, but survived. A year later, he was still reeling from all that happened. During this time of prayer and worship, he went off by himself, feeling tired, fearful, and confused. As Matt tells the story:

> *Knowing Josh had suffered a loss no 12-year-old can easily endure, I walked up behind him and put my hand on his shoulder. He was slouched in his seat, and his face was covered so no one would see him crying. I leaned over to gently speak in his ear and asked, "What's wrong?"*

"I don't know."

I knew that meant I should ask again.

"What's the matter?"

He told me he felt scared, like God was far away from him.

The Holy Spirit quickened me to ask him: "Do you know how close God is?"

"No."

I quickly replied, saying; "He is this close."

I then scooped down and gripped him, putting my arms around him and hugging him as long and as hard as I could.

Josh didn't need my theology or thoughts at that point. He needed a tangible understanding of how much God loves him and how close He really is.

Later that evening, he thanked me and asked, "What do kids do when they feel far from God and don't have a dad to hold them?"

Even in his youth, Josh recognized the need for human touch, for the tangible touch of a father.

One Christmas, a team of five families from Warren, Pennsylvania came to Houston, giving up their own holiday to serve others during our Holiday of Hope ministry and other Christmas outreaches. As one of the dads on the team was helping a five-year-old girl and her mom pick out Christmas toys from our fellowship hall, the little girl looked up to him and said, "Could you give me a hug for my daddy? I don't have a daddy." He hugged her as he tried to hold back his tears.

God depends on us to be that father in the flesh to those who don't have a dad to hold them. Let us not be afraid to impart this intimacy and to "be there," in person and by example. It was no mistake He chose to pass on blessings through the laying on of hands.

6

Daddies, Daughters, and Strength to Deliver

Daddies, Daughters, and Strength to Deliver

When we think of the effects of fatherlessness, we often think in terms of the father-son relationship and the impact on the sons. But we would be remiss in neglecting the detrimental effect the lack of fathers has had on the women in our society.

During a tour of a juvenile justice center, one of our staff members was told that dealing with juvenile girls is among their biggest and fastest growing problems. They're constantly getting in trouble. They're angry, violent, uncontrollable, and mentally unstable.

"You can't put them into a residential facility," he was told. "They'll run away. They're just unruly." There is also a growing trend of juvenile girls involved in gangs.

County officials have identified two primary issues at the heart of all these problems. The first problem is diet. When a person doesn't care about herself or believes no one else does, she doesn't care what she eats. Such people often turn to food for comfort. The second problem is men. Most of the girls have issues with their fathers. They're looking for identity, so they get involved in relationships or gangs. The boys they give their bodies to break their hearts and use them. Sadly, the cycle continues until they feel they have nothing to live for.

Socialization and finding identity are healthy processes, but when the family unit is fragmented, there are no parameters to define the God-given roles of parent, daughter, and sister. Without a place to find identity, young people create their own worlds and families. Sometimes this occurs through gangs. We see it with street kids, too, who create their own family dynamics and even find identity in their "street names."

When there is a breech of covering we feel exposed, vulnerable, and even unwanted. When a woman feels uncovered

When a girl has not experienced the love of a father, she will look for that love by giving herself to men.

by her husband, there is disarray in the home. When a girl feels uncovered by her parents, and especially by her father, she looks elsewhere to find the strength God designed to come from him. She looks for identity in places that are outside the realm of God's intended plan. And when a girl has not experienced the love of a father, she will look for that love by giving herself to men.

One of my daughters in the faith ministers to young women all over the world, but also has an ongoing group that meets in her home. Before Laura's father went to be with Jesus, he asked me to help watch over her and her mother, and now she regards me as a spiritual father.

"A few years ago, the Lord opened my eyes to the desperate need of this generation's young women, and how they need to be spiritually mothered and fathered," Laura says. "I found myself surrounded by the most beautiful, precious young women. They all loved the Lord passionately and wanted nothing more than to please Him. As I developed sweet friendships with these precious souls, I began to hear their stories. To my sad surprise, almost all of them were stories full of woundedness and brokenness."

Laura asked me to speak to the young ladies she mentors, believing I could minister God's heart to heal them from their "daddy issues." I spoke to them with the heart of a father, repented to them on behalf of any men who hurt them, and released them into their destinies by praying over them with a father's blessing.

One of the girls in the group, Adriana, has not seen her biological father since she was five years old:

> *I remember all the adventurous things I did with my father like it was yesterday. He was full of energy when I was five years old and always knew how to plan our day. My day started with my dad dressing me, brushing my hair, and walking me to school. He didn't have to do these things, but he did them because he wanted to. He considered me his pride and joy because I was his only daughter. Our day would end after school when he would pick me up, and we would walk back through a small bayou where I would catch guppies in a sandwich bag. There are so many memories I have of my dad! I never want to lose them because they are all I have.*

> *Life does not always end up the way you would like it, especially when your parents divorce. I never really understood how much of an impact it had on my life until now. For so long, I never cared to know the true story about why he left because I was angry at him, and my mom never knew how to explain, so she left it all unknown.*

> *As the years went by and I grew older, I desired a relationship with him once again. But how do you pick up where*

you left off when someone has been gone since you were five?

I am 24 years old now, and as I replay situations in my life that brought about terrible consequences, I know they are a result of not having my father. I had no male role model, so I ran to men to satisfy that void in my life. Of course, I found myself in relationships with the wrong men. But I was so afraid to be abandoned again that I stayed with them to feel safe and protected. I never knew the difference between a good man and a bad man, I only knew I felt loved and that I belonged to someone. I have been in the worst relationships with physical, emotional and mental abuse, but I stayed, because I thought I needed a man to complete me. If my dad had been around, I don't think I would have gone through these things because a father offers his strength and wisdom to help you choose the right man.

Recently, my dreams of seeing my dad again nearly came true. I was invited to California with a friend, so I accepted in hopes of seeing my dad. I contacted him, and we talked about plans of driving to Fresno to meet him halfway. You can imagine my excitement! I began preparing a photo album with pictures of me growing up and pictures of me now, just to help us catch up. We were expecting to meet him on Friday morning after we flew into San Diego, but the week before I left I could never get an answer when I called him at his house. I left three messages for him.

By Thursday, I realized it was not going to happen, and I was right. I cried, and I began to question why he would do this to me and not even call me. I still do not know the real story, but I know the day will come for me to see him again. It seems to me that 19 years is long enough to wait, but God knows best and I trust His timing to be perfect.

In the meantime, I look back in my life and I see how God has blessed me with my stepfather, who has done so much for my family. I also see how He placed other men of God in my path to stand in the gap as spiritual fathers — men like Pastor Doug Stringer. His words and prayers have blessed me so much, especially when he helped me realize my Father in heaven has been here for me all these years! Even though my biological father was not present to see all the things I have feared and overcome, my Heavenly Father was there holding my hand, giving me all the strength I needed.

I see many similarities in Adriana's testimony and my own. My parents, too, divorced when I was a child. As a young man, I felt the desperate void of his absence. I left my mother and stepfather's house and lived an aimless life for a period, living on freight trains and selling plasma so I could have money to eat.

Eventually, I determined to find my father, and discovered he lived in Houston. I moved here and found him, but it did not fill the void. Like Adriana, the search for my father led me to my Heavenly Father.

But even with the similarities in our testimonies, we must still acknowledge God's design in creating men and women to be different. Our needs are different. Our giftings are different. And our wounds are different. And as the body of Christ, we must respond to women accordingly.

Repentance and Release

Men who are not Christ-like put women in a wrong position, whether they are fathers, husbands, or spiritual authorities. This has a rippling effect across society in the form of oppression, suppression, and all kinds of abuse. Atrocities occur across the globe as women are raped, forced to have abortions, inflicted with mandated traditional rites of passage, and abandoned by irresponsible men. Emptiness, shame, and a sense of unworthiness have hindered many. Women are hurting, and we need to bring healing. They must be released to wholeness in Christ, but this requires repentance on the part of men. We must repent for the sins against women and begin to speak against the injustice toward women around the world.

At the 2001 Global Celebration of Women in Houston, I was ble to stand in the gap of repentance toward the women who attended. "On behalf of all the men who have ever hurt you," I said, "verbally or physically abused you, or even kept you oppressed in the name of religion, please forgive us. Perhaps you've been held back from fulfilling your destiny, or you've been made to feel like a second-class citizen. But ladies, the Lord Himself looks at you and says, 'I have a destiny to accomplish through those who surrender to Me.'"

Many tearful women came to me at the conclusion of the meeting saying, "I finally got set free tonight. I understand that I have a destiny." I reported what happened at this meeting to a ministry friend in Atlanta. She began to cry over the phone saying, "When you shared what you did at that citywide prayer meeting, it set me free."

I delivered a similar message at the 2005 Inspire Women's Rally in Houston where I was privileged to be the first male keynote speaker. Over 2,000 women came together, from a wide variety of denominations and ethnic backgrounds. Afterward, many of the women said they felt like a spiritual father had blessed them and released them to their future.

The more we begin to operate in this prophetic act of repentance, the more we will release the body of Christ to its destiny. The world is desperately searching for answers, and it's going to take both men and women to fulfill God's purposes.

I believe America will experience revival either by a birthing or a shaking. I relate the process we're in to that of a troubled pregnancy in which a woman needs strength to deliver a healthy child. Earlier, we quoted King Hezekiah:

> *"This is a day of trouble and distress because the children are ready to be born but there's no strength to deliver them."*
>
> *-Isaiah 37:3*

We need the Spirit of Christ to empower us!

And not just the women. It's going to take *all* of us to go from death to life, from tragedy to triumph.

Men are meant to be strength-givers to women. Yet for different reasons women have felt vulnerable, forsaken, or in some ways devalued.

For a healthy baby to be born, in the spiritual or the natural, there must be a healthy womb. To have a healthy womb requires a healthy woman. And to have a healthy woman, we need healthy men who are not intimidated by the giftings of women. Those men can and will give her strength to deliver.

Men are meant to be strength-givers to women. Yet for different reasons women have felt vulnerable, forsaken, or in some ways devalued. Men have allowed insecurities and fears to hinder them, and this has created problems that have trickled down through society.

When we men become secure in our identities in Christ, we aren't threatened by the giftings in women. We are able to bless them and release them to become all that God destined them to be.

Proverbs 13:31 says, *"Don't give your strength to women."* This means that men should not abdicate the strength God has given them by stepping out of their roles and leaving women to take on more responsibilities than God intended for them. It means not to be a wimp made in America — or in my case, Japan.

But we cannot go to the other extreme by being harsh and abusive. Jesus is saying, "Don't give away your strength, *be* a strength."

> *If we're going to have a healthy birth and a life-giving, nurturing process for an entire generation, we need to release healthy women to fulfill their destinies.*

Men were designed to guide, protect, encourage, and strengthen women. Women were created to be life-givers and nurturers. So if we're going to have a healthy birth and a life-giving, nurturing process for an entire generation, we need to release healthy women to fulfill their destinies. And we need godly men who are secure in Christ to come alongside as strength-givers so that, together, we will be a powerful, positive force for God's Kingdom.

Jesus Showed the Way

Jesus knew how to strengthen both men and women and release them into their ministries. When He spoke to the Samaritan woman at the well, He went against society's norms in two ways: she was a woman and a Samaritan (John 4). Even the disciples questioned what He was doing. But no one could deny this woman received not only an answer to her questions but also new life. She was affirmed, empowered, and released to proclaim the Good News as she declared, "Come, see a Man!"

Like the Samaritan woman, many women today need

affirmation. Emotional and spiritual barrenness have stripped away the very attributes deposited into women, resulting in a *physically* barren generation, as well.

Women are marrying later in life, establishing careers first and family second. They are approaching their 30s and 40s without bearing children. Many men fear commitment, and their reaction to the women's movement was to pull away from relationships.

We are as desperate today for God to fill our empty wombs as Hannah was for Him to fill hers (1 Samuel 1:11). A barren woman who greatly desired a son, Hannah regularly poured out her heart to God at the altar, reminding Him of her affliction. Once when she was crying out in the house of the Lord, Eli the prophet brought encouragement and gave her hope. When God answered the travail of her heart, Hannah gave birth to a new generation of prophets through her son, Samuel — a generation that would prepare the way for the coming of the Lord (I Samuel 19-20).

There's a new generation of prophets and prophetesses today yet to be born, both in the natural and in the realm of the spirit. They're ready to come forth but we, the church, need strength to deliver them.

Men of God must support, nurture, and encourage the women. Hannah's husband Elkanah represents the type of covering we are to provide. He comforted Hannah, stood by her, and blessed her through her despair and through her labor.

We must undergird the women of our generation. The Valley of Baca, or place of weeping, will become a spring (Psalm 84:6). Streams of living water will gush forth, providing a lasting drink to those who are thirsty.

The well where Jesus met the Samaritan woman was not just any watering place. It was Jacob's well, and from it sprang living waters that quenched the thirsts of generations. As the women of our day receive the same revelation and freedom as the Samaritan woman, their night of weeping will cease. And together the body of Christ will declare, "Come, see a Man!"

Birthing a Generation

Our world needs a birthing of resurrection life that will lead to revival and a harvest of thousands upon thousands of souls. Something is getting ready to happen, and we need to PUSH—Pray Until Something Happens—for the release of a generation living on the edge for Christ: men, women, and children together, becoming all God wants them to be.

God needs all of us - regardless of race, status, age, or gender - to orchestrate His will upon the earth. Both men and women are needed for prayer and spiritual warfare. Galatians 3:28 says,

"There is neither Jew nor Greek, there is neither slave nor free, there is neither male nor female; for you are all one in Christ Jesus."

We need the passion and zeal of the young; the life-giving, nurturing nature of women; and the strong, protective, and empowering attributes of men. To give birth to revival, we need to combine the gifts and strengths of the whole army of God.

God needs all of us - regardless of race, status, age, or gender - to orchestrate His will upon the earth.

It's time for us to rise up with the radical determination and conviction of Joan of Arc. She was an inexperienced warrior whose enthusiasm inspired the entire French army, something no king had been able to do. During battle she approached the general of the army, stating emphatically, "I'm going to lead the men over the wall."

The general replied, "There isn't one man who is going to follow you."

With her eyes fixed like flint, 17-year-old Joan replied, "I wouldn't know. I don't plan on looking back to check." She took off over the wall, and every one of the men followed. Her courageous example delivered her country.[1]

Birthing revival will require Joan's style of heroism and radical commitment in the hearts of those who bear the Gospel of good news today.

Just as Jesus approached the Samaritan woman at the well, He's approaching you and me. The challenges, barriers, and limitations placed on us are now in the past. It's time for the Lord to heal us.

He's not ashamed to call you His child. He's not embarrassed by who you are. He created you in His image. Release your past, and run with the vision God has placed on your heart. He has a purpose for your life.

If we allow Him to change our hearts, a healthy birth will follow. And after the baby is born, we'll forget the pain, the sorrow, and the obstacles. We'll rejoice in what the Lord has done (John 16:20-22).

Identifying the strengths of each generation and each gender, we'll become what I term Gen-Edge people—a generation living on the edge for Christ. Functioning in God's design and order, we'll all benefit as we benefit His kingdom.

It's Time to Have a Baby!

God is calling His people to become fathers to the fatherless and husbands to the widows. He is calling men to rise up and be men, to accept their God-given positions in the family and in the church by providing strength. He wants men of strength, maturity, and integrity to be spiritual fathers to sons and daughters. He is calling us forth!

God is giving strength to birth the coming revival. He is birthing a fresh generation with a fresh anointing out of the spiritual womb of His church. They will be a prophetic generation that will not be like the former generations. They will not be like their fathers.

"That the generation to come might know them the children who would be born, that they may arise and declare them to their children, that they may set their hope in God, and not forget the works of God, but keep His commandments; and may not be like their fathers, a stubborn and rebellious generation, a generation that did not set its heart aright, and whose spirit was not faithful to God."

-Psalm 78:6-8

Instead of being stubborn and rebellious, they will be a generation putting their hope in God, not succombing to compromise, and living on the edge for Jesus .

God is ready to bring forth a massive move through the lives of His people. It won't be contained in any one denomination, church building, or even one nation. He is doing something exponential. He has put that plan within our spiritual wombs, and is giving us the strength to bring it forth. Unfulfilled visions, dreams, and passions that have been locked away for a long time will now come to birth. Not only are we in labor to bring forth a prophetic generation, we are in the process of bringing the fullness of His church to birth, as well.

God is giving strength to birth the coming revival. He is birthing a fresh generation with a fresh anointing out of the spiritual womb of His church.

It's time for me, and it's time for you. Get ready to birth a lasting revival that will change our world.

As a man of God I come to you with a word of encourage-ment—the same one the prophet Eli proclaimed to Hannah: *"Go in peace, and the God of Israel grant your petition which you have asked of Him"* (1 Samuel 1:17).

Fulfill your destiny and be part of the beautiful birth of a prophetic generation. We're in labor, and it's time to have a baby!

7

A Church God Can Use

A Church God Can Use

I met Peter and Wes, members of the Newsboys music group, when I was asked to speak at a Houston celebration. We sat together at a pre-event pastors' luncheon and soon discovered a mutual passion to invest in the younger generation.

Over the past ten years, they told me, the Newsboys have ministered to more than ten million young people at their concerts. God has given them a burden now to go beyond just pointing youth to Christ, but also building in them a strong foundation. To do that, the Newsboys are partnering with Every Nation Ministries to produce *The Purple Book: A Foundational Bible Study for Building Strong Disciples.*

The book includes a letter from Peter that says, "...although I grew up in the church, a lot of these foundational principles were not grounded in my life. Memorize and meditate on the Scriptures daily, and teach others to do the same. Together, we will make this generation a people full of the knowledge of God's Word — a people with a strong foundation worth handing down to the next generation." [1]

The church that will experience true revival is the one who presents herself as the Servant Bride, the one who is willing to serve the Lord and willing to serve those dirty, smelly, thirsty camels coming out of the wilderness of life.

God wants to heal this generation and set them free, but we must first learn what the Newsboys have learned. We must not only share the Gospel with them boldly, we must also go the extra mile to help them grow strong in the faith and reach out to others with the love of God.

Sparks of revival are flickering throughout our land and throughout the world. But the church that will experience true revival is the one who presents herself as the Servant Bride, the one who is willing to serve the Lord and willing to serve those dirty, smelly, thirsty camels coming out of the wilderness of life.

The Extra Mile

On any given day, I'll get voice messages at the office from street kids we helped in the early days of the ministry. "This is your son Jeremy calling. I'm hanging in there. Keep praying for me. I love you, man." "This is Jamie. My daughter Angel just graduated from kindergarten. Tell everybody I said hello." "This is Lance. Let Doug know I'm doing OK. I'm going to church and serving in a soup kitchen." "This is Kevin. Could you send me a Bible?"

When we launched our ministry we were a radical group of young people, untrained and uneducated, but with a passion to win the lost. We took people into our homes. We went the extra mile. At one time, I had 17 people staying in my apartment, many of them just like those camels: dirty, thirsty, and smelly. But God gave us hearts to serve them.

At the annual banquet for Montrose Street Reach, a young man shared his testimony. Raised in a fatherless home and sexually abused at a young age, he had been living on the streets of Houston as a transvestite prostitute who called himself Olivia. Looking beyond his confused exterior, the ministry's leaders saw him through the eyes of God and pursued him relentlessly. It literally took years, but God's love and persistence finally broke through, and he gave his life to Christ. Today, he lives with a family from a local church and works on the church staff, where he is being nurtured and educated in the ways of God. Where would this young man be if Montrose Street Reach and the churches serving with them had not been willing to persevere?

Buddy and Carolyn had seen God move in radical ways in the lives of young people during the 1970s and 1980s. With retirement approaching, they served a large church in Humble, Texas, where Buddy was pastor. They were well taken care of financially, but their hearts were burdened with a passion for the young people of the community. They could no longer be content with "business as usual."

Teaming with their daughter and son-in-law, Shari and Mike, they purchased a city block in old downtown Humble where they built a skate park, turned an old gas station into a cyber café called Fuel, and started Somebody Cares Humble. Secular bands come from all over the area to play at Fuel, even though they have to sign a contract not to drink, swear, or sing lyrics that are inappropriate and ungodly.

Local teens work and serve in the café and the skate-park. They earn college scholarships if they keep up their grades and stay clean from alcohol and drugs. The church has become a youth church called Pipeline, pastored by Mike and Shari. Hundreds of kids have been spiritually fathered in the ministry through what we have termed "pre-conversion discipleship." Many of these kids would be heading directly down a path of destruction if not for the sacrifice and commitment of this family.

There are so many others out there doing the same — going the extra mile.

Tony got out of Bible college and began doing street ministry in the Deep Ellum area of Dallas. With the purchase of a popular coffee-house called "Insomnia," hundreds of young people from the Goth and other sub-cultures received ministry on a regular basis, once again through "pre-conversion discipleship." Though they no longer own the coffee-house, the ministry is now called "Life in Deep Ellum" and has expanded its outreach to the entire community.

J.J. is a spiritual son in the Lord living and working in College Station, just north of Houston. SOS Ministries reaches out to young people and college students in the area with weekly Bible studies and transitional living for kids who have nowhere else to go. Saved by the Lord from a life of crime and gangs, J.J.'s heart is that no young life should slip through the cracks. "In a man's life and ministry, I believe he must be pointed out by great men of faith," J.J. wrote to me once. "Even Jesus was pointed out by His Father. You, Doug, came and pointed me out." Now, he is doing the same for his own spiritual children.

SOS now partners with Stuart, a medical doctor who heads up Medical Missions International, as Somebody Cares Brazos Valley. Stuart's ministry was birthed when God spoke to him during one of my Bible studies to use his medical giftings to help people in Africa.

In Stafford, Texas, God gave EZ and Lena a vision for young people years ago, and through that vision they started Generation Jesus. Today, the ministry is equipping a radical group of young people to impact the community through their church, called The Epicenter.

Gideon and Sara minister to Asian Indians and other young

people at Houston Baptist University. Jeremy heads up Generation Xcel and coordinated the youth outreach for Billy Graham's New York City Crusade. Mike launched the Firehouse Cyber Café with a vision to have it open 24 hours a day so young people would always have a place to go.

And let's not forget those rescuing lives through the literal adoption of babies and children. In 2001, there were 800 adoptable children in the Harris County, Texas, foster care system. Somebody Cares Houston spearheaded "Hope in Houston," an adoption awareness campaign.

> *In 2001, there were 800 adoptable children in the Harris County, Texas, foster care system.*

YWAM Houston, who oversaw the campaign for us, has continued the vision through the opening of an adoption agency in our offices. One of the first adoptions was the baby of a street kid from Houston's Montrose area. That child was adopted by the daughter and son-in-law of Buddy and Carolyn, who work with Somebody Cares, Humble, Texas. Buddy and Carolyn ministered to street kids in Montrose in the 1970s, and now their first grandchild is a fruit of seeds they planted years ago.

Others, too, have stepped to the plate. Henry and Delia served in our ministry for many years, and adopted a foster child. The Byerleys actually inspired our awareness campaign. When Mr. Bylerley first came to me, he and his wife had 17 children—ten of their own, and seven adopted. "If you don't do something to get the word out about the foster children who need to be adopted," he said to me, "my wife is going to adopt all 800 of them!"

Going the extra mile does not come without a price. The Byerleys are not wealthy people, and their actions are motivated solely and literally from a good heart. These kids are from troubled backgrounds. Many times, the Byerleys' hearts are broken by the very young people they've sacrificed to help. Yet they have persevered and laid a foundation in the lives of these children so that when the storms of life come, they have an opportunity to stand on the rock of Jesus Christ.

We've seen our street kids and others die tragically, through AIDS, drive-by shootings, and gang-related violence. Brandy, for example, was a prostitute who died of AIDS. We arranged and conducted a funeral for her and paid for the burial because she had no family to claim her. Hollywood was a street kid who used to say, "I own these streets." The day before he died from a shooting he said to a friend, "I need to get my life right with God."

We've grieved over the premature loss of these lives, yet we know they at least had a chance to call on the name of the Lord. *The greater tragedy is not that these lives were lost, but that so many lives are lost without the opportunity to hear the good news of the Gospel. Many of them go through life not knowing where to turn in the tough times.*

Today's generation is hungry for love. But are we willing to work with those we consider unlovely? Are we willing to feed them?

> *Today's generation is hungry for love. But are we willing to work with those we consider unlovely?*

Will we go the extra mile with them? Will we adopt them, either in the spiritual or in the natural? All too often, the church does not take seriously its responsibility to parent a generation. We give them a lot of fluff, but no spiritual substance. They need to know, when times get tough, they can call "911 Heaven" and connect directly to their Father.

God is challenging us to get out of our comfort zones and reach out to the camels coming out of the wilderness. More than this, we must be willing to go the distance with them. God loves them, and with the same love in which He reached out to us, we must have a heart to reach out to them.

Rivers of Revival

There is an orphaned and father-less generation living within a nation that has been "divorced" from its godly foundations. But that very generation will see God's grace pour out in one of the greatest revivals we have ever seen. Why? Because God Himself will adopt this generation.

Nothing can hinder the purposes of God. This generation will be the group in which the exponential anointings of the Old Testament will converge, thus preparing a people to go forth into their destinies as they prepare the way for the coming of the Lord. God intends to release a massive outpouring of His Spirit that will transcend every denominational and ethnic background—a sustainable awakening—through a young generation. We, the church, must come alongside them and stand with them.

There is an orphaned and fatherless generation living within a nation that has been "divorced" from its godly foundations.

God will not judge the world today as in Noah's days, but instead desires His spotless Bride to be an ark of refuge for a world seeking safety. In so doing, from the womb to the youth, there will be an army of laborers released into the kingdom of God.

> *Your people shall be volunteers In the day of Your power;*
> *In the beauties of holiness, from the womb of the morning,*
> *You have the dew of Your youth.*
>
> *-Psalm 110:3*

God will take this generation and cause them to impact every element of culture and sub-culture, from media to arts to education to business. They will sign up as volunteers for God's Army, to serve the Lord in love and compassion to the nations.

In Zechariah 2, the Bible says there will be such a move of God that the church walls will not contain it—like trying to contain a fire burning wider and wider, gathering more and more people. God's wall of fire will burn away the chaff and purify a people who are willing to consecrate themselves before Him.

The church God is looking for is one that is already serving a hurting generation. God can pour out His Spirit on that kind of church.

Accepting Who God Sends

Peter Ferrara, associate professor of law at George Mason University School of Law in Northern Virginia wrote:

However, that very generation that will see God's grace pour out in one of the greatest revivals we have ever seen. Why? Because God Himself will adopt this generation.

"*An American is English, or French, or Italian, Irish, German, Spanish, Polish, Russian or Greek. An American may also be Mexican, African, Indian, Chinese, Japanese, Australian, Iranian, Asian, or Arab, or Pakistani, or Afghan.*"[2]

I'm proud of my Asian heritage, but I'm not Japanese first. I'm an American. But even above that, I'm a Christian. I have the blood of Jesus pumping through me now and so my identity is with the body of Christ. We may be colored differently on the outside, but we all have the same Spirit on the inside. Our common identity is in Jesus.

The Bible says we are to run the race to obtain all He has for us, and I'm of the "obtaining race!" I stand with my brothers and sisters in Christ and look toward the upward call of God with a common identity.

Hatred and racism are more rampant than ever through-out the world, and division is commonplace. But in the house of the Lord, a true last-days revival will include people from all nations. It will happen when we put aside differences, lay down our weapons, and gather at the house of the Lord, declaring, "We are brothers and sisters, we love God, and we love one another" (see Micah 4:3)

This generation may come with earrings in their eyebrows and earrings in their noses and earrings in their foreheads, from every color, every nation, every race. They may be outcast, lame, and sick. They may have stinky breath or matted hair. It doesn't matter. They're coming in, they're thirsty and hungry, and we must choose to serve them. As we do, God will change their nature and transform their lives, and they will become the prophetic generation He intended them to be. But it's up to us have that spirit of serving and to allow them to gather at the mountain of the Lord.

The principles in God's Word can be applied to any generation—they transcend generational barriers. But we must be willing to accept the differences in each generation. Their styles of worship, dress, music, and behaviors may not be what we are accustomed to, but we must see them through God's eyes and love them unconditionally. We must adopt them and welcome them into our family with open arms.

We must adopt them and welcome them into our family with open arms.

Adrienne S. Gaines writes, in "The Joshua Generation":

"'Generation Y' is surprising some observers as they demonstrate a unique willingness to build friendship and community with people of all racial backgrounds. Indeed, this group of young men and women, born after 1982, are more cross-cultural from birth — many are from mixed ra-

cial heritage and 36 percent are 'non-white,' according to Millennials Rising: The Next Great Generation by Neil Howe and William Strauss (Vintage). Though they've been described by the media as materialistic and spoiled, as Christians, they are quickly answering the call to impact our cities — and the world — for Christ. Many of their predecessors, the Generation Xers, have emerged as ministry leaders, acting as Moses to this group of courageous Joshuas. But will they take us into the Promised Land on the issue of Biblical unity? Hope springs eternal."[3]

God is going to pour out His Spirit upon all flesh, and we will see a radical "John the Baptist generation" raised up who will do mighty exploits for God. Are we willing to serve them? Are we willing to accept them for who they are, "as is," without judgment and with no strings attached? Are we willing to invite them in regardless of their backgrounds? God sees our potential, and if we are to love as Christ loved, He is calling us to do the same to others.

God calls His church into unity. The Father summons us to accept whatever "camels" He sends our way, regardless of their pasts, their appearances, and their ethnicities. The church needs to accept whomever He sends.

It's risky, requiring sacrifice. We must face our own prejudices and fears. If we're willing to allow God to deal with our concerns and prejudices, we can become the kind of church upon whom He can pour His Spirit like never before.

Learning From our Pasts

God wants us to learn from our pasts. He wants to use the wounds of the generations who have gone before us to help shield the generations coming behind us. But before we can understand how to function in our anointings, purposes, and identities, we must first know where we have gone wrong. We must uproot the old that is bad while planting and nurturing that which is right.

The truth is, we have the crisis of fatherlessness in America, but we all have to take responsibility for our own choices. We can claim to be dysfunctional, co-dependent, and victimized. We can base these claims on upbringing, environment or societal pressures. Eventually, however, we have to take responsibility and no longer play the blame game. Once we recognize we need help, we can make a choice to live for the future.

The Bible says in Ezekiel 18:2, *"The fathers have eaten sour grapes, and the children's teeth are set on edge."* Later, Jeremiah 31:29-30 says:

> *"In those days they shall say no more: 'The fathers have eaten sour grapes, and the children's teeth are set on edge.' But every one shall die for his own iniquity; every man who eats the sour grapes, his teeth shall be set on edge."*

This is basically acknowledging that the sins of the fathers truly do affect their children, but it's no excuse for the children to disobey. Everyone must answer for their own sin and stop blaming their fathers for their personal evils and flaws.

We can't change our pasts. But we can understand that the choices we make every day determine our future. We need to take responsibility.

My friend Roger served in Viet Nam and, within mere minutes, was blasted by a hand grenade, shot twice, bayoneted, then left to die. He was rushed to a MASH unit, where the medical team said there was little chance he'd live. If he did live, they said, it would be without some of his limbs. Gangrene was setting in, and amputation would be required. On top of that, Roger had 72 shrapnel wounds, and his face was swollen with infection.

In spite of it all, Roger began to recover. Every day, each one of his 72 wounds was opened up and scrubbed to make sure the infection was not progressing. If the wounds were left to heal on their own, they would become infected. The pain, he said, was unbearable. Though he could not speak, he cried to God from his heart: "God, if there is a God, if You let me live, I'll serve You the rest of my life."

God's grace poured out on Roger as he made that simple cry. Slowly the wounds healed, until one day the infection was completely gone. Soon the pain was gone as well, and all that remained were the scars. Roger not only survived, but was restored completely. Without God's grace, Roger said, he wouldn't have made it.

We, too, can have memories and scars, but we don't have to hang on to the pain.

We, too, can have memories and scars, but we don't have to hang on to the pain. We can cry out to God, and He will heal us in His infinite grace. The pain we cling to can hold us back from God's greater purposes.

Jesus was able to look beyond the suffering of the cross and find the joy set before Him, says Hebrews 12:2. We must be able to see beyond our circumstances and look to God's future. The only way to receive healing is to let go of the past.

Hope and Consequences

I have met many people who have suffered because of their own choices and the impact their parent's choices had on their lives. I recall one young man who became a part of our ministry for several years. When John was a teenager, he became heavily involved in drugs. He later accepted Jesus Christ as His Savior, but soon returned to a life of drug addiction. During that season, he contracted AIDS.

When we met him just a few years later, John had been given six months to live. He returned to a relationship with Jesus and, by God's grace, lived an additional three years. During that time, he participated in 14 mission trips and spoke to many at-risk youth and young adults about the choices they were making. He was a faithful intercessor for the ministry and for me personally. Though this man's life was cut short due to the consequences of his actions, he had found hope, meaning and purpose. His life left a legacy to the glory of God!

The generation outside the walls of the church looks messed up. The world has labeled them dysfunctional. They are regarded as permanently and terminally co-dependent and hopeless. They are not permitted to claim victory as they are taught mantras, like, "once an alcoholic, always an alcoholic, " "once a drug addict, always an addict," and many more.

But *my* Bible says in 2 Corinthians 5:17 that all things pass away and become new in Christ. I am a new creature in Him! I may still struggle with temptation, but I am now aware of my struggles and know that God will give me the strength to overcome.

Genuine freedom comes from being secure in Him. The Bible says in Galatians 5:1, *"Stand fast therefore in the liberty by which Christ has made us free, and do not be entangled again with a yoke of bondage."* I am free from bondage, and I am alive in Christ.

And in that place of freedom, the pain from my past is gone. The scars still remain, but the pain does not. God healed me so I am able to operate in His fullness. I can't use my past as a cop-out or an excuse, but I can acknowledge

God has converted the pain from my past into compassion— and with that compassion, I am equipped to love the unlovable.

where I've come from. God has converted the pain from my past into compassion—and with that compassion, I am equipped to love the unlovable.

God is looking for those who will make themselves available, who will say, "Here am I, send me." He searches for those who have learned from their pasts, who take responsibility for their mistakes, who will accept who He sends, who will go the extra mile. That is the kind of church God can use to father a generation of orphans, emerging from the wilderness.

8

The Rock of ALL Ages

The Rock of ALL Ages

Returning from a ministry trip to Fiji, I stopped in Denver for a few days. At the airport there I saw a father with his young son, who was wearing a t-shirt that read, "My daddy rocks!"

At that tender age, this child's world revolved around his daddy. But as I remembered myself at that age I was reminded of how my trust with my own father had been severed. I wondered how long it would last for that little boy. As the years go on, will this dad provide the acceptance, approval, and affirmation his son will need? Will he be able to withstand the storms of life in such a way that his son will grow up feeling safe, secure, and protected? Will this son be able to stand on the trust and intimacy he now experiences with his dad, or will his dad respond to the cares of this world in such a way that, instead, it rocks this little boy's world?

I thought of James Boswell, the biographer of the great British author, Samuel Johnson. (The story is sometimes attributed to Johnson's life but, nonetheless, it is a stirring story with a profound point.) As a boy, James once spent the day on a fishing trip with his father. He recorded that memorable event in his journal by simply stating, "Today I went fishing with my dad. It was the greatest day of my life!"

> *How difficult it is when children discover their fathers' perception of this pivotal relationship is so very different from their own. This meeting of perception with reality can become a turning point for any child.*

Boswell's father was an influential and busy man, so this day of intentional attention spoke volumes into the life of this young boy. Years later, he came across his father's journal after his father had died. He remembered that day with fondness and wondered what his father had recorded about their time together. He discovered his father's perception of that day had been very different from his own. "Today I went fishing with my son," he wrote. "It was a day wasted."[1]

What an impact the love of a father has on a child's life and how devastating when it is lacking! What hurt it brings to a child's tender heart when the father has no time for his little one. How difficult it is when children discover their fathers' perception of this pivotal relationship is so very different from their own. This meeting of perception with reality can become a turning point for any child. It's the time when the child will continue to say "my daddy rocks" or the reality of a severed relationship will rock his very foundation.

I contrast that to a story from one of my own spiritual sons. Ruben's father was killed when he was five years old. He carried a deep wound within him that expressed itself by seeking acceptance, approval, and affirmation. After he came to the Lord, he became a part of our ministry, where he came to know the healing power of his Heavenly Father.

Years later, I entrusted Ruben with a challenging project in which he was in charge of a city-wide outreach event with several major athletes, businessmen, ministry leaders, and even Hollywood producers. His responsibilities included meeting with pastors and with leaders from local schools, representing the ministry at meetings of business leaders, identifying children from needy families with vision and hearing problems, and coordinating a number of volunteers to box up free food that would be given to the families. He was also involved in media interviews and several other critical tasks.

The event culminated with the national premier of a Hollywood movie at a Houston theatre. During the evening, Ruben's 21-year-old son, Chris, had the opportunity to introduce himself to some of the business and ministry leaders his dad had been working with.

"My name is Chris. I'm Ruben's son," he said proudly, to which each individual inevitably replied by saying how much they appreciated Ruben, what a great job he had done with the outreach, and how well he represented Somebody Cares.

Later, as Chris looked around and considered all that had occurred — hundreds of children with new hearing aids and eyeglasses walking down a red carpet like celebrities, families getting free groceries, television cameras and newspaper reporters — he said to his mother, "You know what? My dad rocks!"

Even through years of watching his family go through life's struggles, trials and difficulties, this grown son — now a student at a Christian university — can still say, "My dad rocks!" His own dad received healing from his Heavenly Father through the Spirit of Adoption and was able to build his family on the one true foundation, which is *the* rock, Jesus Christ.

The Gen-Edge Miracle

Jesus is the rock of *all* ages and His Father — our Heavenly Father — is the Father of *all generations*. He is a multi-generational God.

He desires the bridging of all generations, identifying the strengths of each and linking them in a common purpose. Once the strengths of each generation are sanctified and brought together, the result will be a force to be reckoned with that will fan the flames for revival like we've never, ever seen.

> *The younger generation needs the wisdom and dreams of an older generation to accomplish their destinies.*
>
>

In Joel 2 and Acts 2, the Bible says "old men shall dream dreams" and "young men shall see visions." The inference is that the older generation will have dreams yet to be accomplished, but they cannot be accomplished unless the passion, zeal, and vision of a younger generation are applied to them. But on the other hand, the younger generation needs the wisdom and dreams of an older generation to accomplish their destinies.

In Scripture, King David had a dream to build a glorious temple, a house for God. His desire was good, but God said the temple would be built by David's son Solomon. Knowing his son would be young and inexperienced, David began laying out the plans God had placed on his own heart so his son would have something on which to build. Solomon entered into the labor of the temple with his father's blessing along with his wisdom.

In May, 2006, I was invited to Australia by one of my sons in the faith, Andrew Merry. I was to preach two weeks of revival services in the Geelong area of the Bellarine Peninsula. In 1983, I had picked up Andrew while he was hitchhiking through Houston. Through a series of "divine mishaps," Andrew stayed in my home and came to know Jesus as his Savior. He went on to pastor a significant Baptist church in the area, and he considers me a spiritual father.

The group of pastors from various denominations in the region who invited me had fasted for 40 days before my arrival. Some of them I had met the first time I visited Australia 20 years earlier. During one of the meetings for pastors and leaders, some told how they had come to know the Lord through our ministry. Others said they looked to me as a spiritual covering. A few years earlier, during another visit, some of them said they see me as a Charles Finney in the area. Although I don't see myself that way, I was very humbled and encouraged. It has been one of my prayers since the beginning of the ministry to have the passion and anointing of a Charles Finney, to impact the community and see people stay true to their Father.

As I was concluding one of the revival services held at Ocean Grove Fellowship, I called forward all the pastors, leaders, ministry workers, and elders I had met on my trips throughout the years, and I had them face the audience. Then I looked out at the spectators and asked, "How many of you are 30 and younger?" As they stood, facing the generation that had been laboring before them, I said, "Behold your fathers and mothers."

Then I addressed my peers, the "young people" of 20 years ago, as they looked out at this awesome group of "younger" people. I called them the "dreamers" of Joel 2 and Acts 2. "Behold your sons and daughters," I said to them.

> *"Think of all those years ago, when you were full of passion and zeal and nothing could stop you! Then you hit challenges. Today, you feel the effects of the physical wear and tear, the emotional wear and tear, the setbacks, the disappointments, the broken and shattered dreams."*
> As they stood face to face, generation to generation, I continued:

"Maybe you feel like you've failed or like your life has been in vain. But look! Your life has not been in vain! Behold this emerging generation of visionaries, full of zeal and passion and uniqueness! THIS is what you've labored for! Your dreams shall be accomplished and fulfilled, through this new generation of prophets and prophetesses! You didn't fail! And your dreams have not died! They're still alive! They will be accomplished! Be encouraged with the passion and zeal of the youth and their uniqueness. Come alongside them, give strength and wisdom, give them strength to deliver!"

To the "visionaries," the young people, I said: "You're not alone! We recognize your uniqueness, and we are here to cover you and give you strength to come forth into your destinies!"

It was a powerful demonstration of the multi-generational blessing God wants to impart to His people. The emerging generation realized they need the former. The former generation was able get their focus off their own journeys and look now to the emerging generation with hope and expectation that their dreams would yet be fulfilled.

Redeeming Our Mistakes

The "baby boomers" have been tagged as a generation of greed. They constituted the hippie era, but were also regarded as the "me generation." As their radicalism was tempered, the boomers became the yuppies. These "upwardly mobile" young adults enjoyed success and prosperity, but morally they fell short. In 1973, with the Roe vs. Wade Supreme Court decision, they became the generation that aborted its babies under the state's sanction, enabling them to abdicate responsibility for their actions. There seemed to be no consequences for their actions, and "doing your own thing" was never easier.

Fast-forward to the generation that followed. They paid dearly for the errors of those who went before. The right to pray had been removed from their schools. They lacked spirituality and identity. Many became fatherless and orphaned, with a large percentage growing up in homes with absentee fathers. The boomers left a generation with an identity crisis in the wake of its selfish living.

The boomers left a generation with an identity crisis in the wake of its selfish living.

According to an article in *Continental Airlines Magazine*, three million of the 78 million baby boomers turned 60 in 2001. This article went on to say, "[they] want more spiritual enrichment in retirement along with simplicity, and they are willing to downsize to get it."[2] They have tried what the world has to offer and found it lacking. Bradley Creed, Ph.D., a Samford University professor of religion, was quoted in the November 2001 issue of *Reader's Digest New Choices* magazine as saying, "Baby boomers are deeply concerned with self-actualization and spiritual growth."[3]

God has grace, and we can learn from the mistakes and errors of the past. Even through these issues, many baby boomers have found the wisdom of God and their redemptive value in the dreams God gives them, even those yet to be realized. Through their failures and years of frustration and searching, those who've found the Lord Jesus Christ and a relationship with the Heavenly Father now have wisdom to share with the next generation.

Jeremy from Generation Xcel understands this well. At our ministry's "think tank" for emerging leaders in 2004, he said, "As an emerging generation, it is very important that we recognize we would not be able to do anything without the men and women of the older generation who have gone before and are leading us through their wisdom. We must honor those who have gone before

The current younger generation has great passion, zeal and vision. As they become sanctified and released into their destinies, they need the covering, wisdom, and strength of the previous generations.

us. We don't want a generation who hands us the checkbook and leaves us. We need our spiritual fathers!"

The current younger generation has great passion, zeal, and vision. As they become sanctified and released into their destinies, they need the covering, wisdom, and strength of the previous generations. They do not need the wisdom that quenches their zeal and passion, but that true wisdom that empowers, strengthens, encourages, and releases the younger generations into their destinies. Then we will see the dreams of the older accomplished through the vision and passion of the younger.

Bridging the Gap

I am part of what I call the "cusp generation," the group at the tail end of the hippie movement and the beginning of the yuppie movement. We were too young to take prayer out of schools, but we were given the responsibility of the fallout. Though I was too young to be a real hippie, I experienced the outcome—the walk-outs from school, long hair, LSD, marijuana, the legacies of the "me generation."

My age group was stuck between two generations. I was not in the group who laid the foundation for these things, I was simply a by-product of it. I have one foot in the "turn on-tune in-drop out" generation, to borrow the phrase coined by Timothy Leary in the 1960s. Yet my other foot is in a whole new generation of crisis, the one consumed with trying to find success: the yuppie generation. Our generation was looking to accomplish greatness by fulfilling our personal needs at the expense of others. As Dr. Cole used to say, "Love desires to give at the expense of self, but lust desires to get at the expense of others."

But God can use those of us who are "stuck in the middle again." We have learned much from having one foot in one generation and the other foot in another. We can be the bridge that connects those who have gone before us with those who follow us. Because we are able to relate to both generations, we can become a bridge-building, peace-making, ambassador generation. We can link the older generation with its wisdom and dreams to younger generation with its vision and passion.

A 2001 *U.S. News and World Report* article reported that "demographers anticipate the boomer generation will rewrite what it means to be a senior citizen. They'll take tai chi classes in their 90s, start second careers at 60, and begin romances at ages that will bring frowns to the foreheads of their grandkids."[4]

Aging boomers are roller-blading, skydiving, and looking for things to keep them in touch with their youth. Yet the very things boomers are looking for are the things the X and Y generations already have! The older generations are trying to live on the edge, and the younger ones already are. The generation gap is not as big as some may think.

> *The older generations are trying to live on the edge, and the younger ones already are.*

Yet it does exist. Not only have the baby boomers generally failed to appreciate or honor the prior generations, they have also viewed the younger generations with contempt. The boomers have pasted derogatory labels on the younger generations, suggesting they are lazy, unmotivated, and good-for-nothing. Instead of trying to get to know them, we have often stood at a distance and shaken our heads with scorn, asking, "Can anything good come from this generation?"

But this is not God's intention. God is multi-generational, and He wants to bridge the generation gaps. He desires unity among all age groups to fulfill His purpose upon the earth.

"God wants to take the wisdom of the old, the resources of the middle generation, and the zeal of the young generation to bring revival," says Mark from BloodNFire Ministries of San Antonio, one of our Somebody Cares affiliates in that city.

The enemy, he says, uses two things to stop revolution. "First, we despise the old, which means we lose the opportunity to glean from their wisdom. Then we look at the young generation and despise them as they are inventing and creating. If we can maintain unity in the midst of diversity, we can maintain the synergism necessary!"

When God called Jeremiah into his prophetic ministry, Jeremiah responded by saying, *"Ah, Lord GOD! Behold, I cannot speak, for I am a youth."* God answered, *"Do not say, 'I am a youth,' for you shall go to all to whom I send you, and whatever I command you, you shall speak"* (Jeremiah 1:6-7).

Age is irrelevant to God. He doesn't want the generations separated.

Age is irrelevant to God. He doesn't want the generations separated. It is time for restoration and the realization that we need each other. As we learned in the last decade to cross racial and denominational lines to become part of something bigger than ourselves, so the generational lines must be crossed as well. Then we can link in fulfilling God's purposes for all the generations.

God is calling us to realize a destiny none of us can accomplish alone. With the dreams and wisdom of the older generation bridged by the cusp generation and linked with the younger generation's vision, passion, and zeal, we can all be released as a generation living on the edge for Christ. We can be part of the "Gen-Edge" miracle!

Each generation is looking to live on that cutting edge. They're all trying to fill the longing of their hearts and souls. In Christ, the yearnings of every generation will be fulfilled. Living on the edge of eternity for Christ is the greatest extreme sport, the greatest experience we could ever have!

Part III

My Daddy Rocks!

9

The Father of ALL Nations

You said, Ask and I'll give the nations to you
O Lord, that's the cry of my heart
Distant shores and the islands will see
Your light, as it rises on us
O Lord, I ask for the nations[1]

-Reuben Morgan

The Father of ALL Nations

Each time I hear this song by Hillsong of Australia, quoting the prayer of David in Psalm 2:8, I get choked up. I believe this is a cry of our generations. It is a promise of God that He *will* give us the nations, because He is the Father of all nations—all we have to do is ask.

> *Ask of Me, and I will give You*
> *The nations for Your inheritance,*
> *And the ends of the earth for Your possession.*
> *-Psalm 2:8*

My friend Suliasi invited me to minister in Fiji for the first time in 1993. At that time, he was director of Every Home for Christ Fiji, a group of passionate young people committed to taking the Gospel to every single home on the Fiji Islands. Their plan was to do it not just once, but three times. Some even made vows not to marry until they accomplished the mission. People thought they were crazy. But they did it, and God has honored them for their faithfulness.

Today, Suliasi pastors one of the largest churches in the Southern Hemisphere. It's located in Suva, Fiji. When I go there and I see the flags from every nation displayed throughout the sanctuary, I am reminded that God is the Father of all nations and all generations. Suliasi's mission has never changed: His desire is to reach the nations, his passion is the Great Commission. After all these years, the cry of his heart remains, "Lord, give me the nations!" That has become the cry of those who are part of his church movement, as well.

Because of seeds planted over the years by Suliasi and others, Fiji has been impacted dramatically by the hand of God.

Because of seeds planted over the years by Suliasi and others, Fiji has been impacted dramatically by the hand of God. You can see the Lord's fingerprints wherever you go. There are documented stories of miraculous healings, not just physical healings but ecological healings—barren trees now producing fruit, stagnant lagoons teeming with fish, poison waters now fresh and clean. Many political leaders and tribal chiefs profess Jesus as Lord. Even villages that once practiced cannibalism now lift up the name of Jesus.

During a visit there in 2006, I had been in Suva as a participant and speaker the Sentinel Group's Global Summit. Suliasi had invited me to preach at his church that Sunday morning, then I moved to a hotel in the city of Nadi (pronounced "Nandee") to be closer to the international airport. I could literally walk out the back door of my hotel room and be on the beach, but instead I was inside working. There were floods back home in Houston, and a fire had just destroyed the warehouse of one of our ministry partners. I was wondering if I should cut my trip short and go home early. In addition to that, I was frustrated with computer problems. Suddenly, out of nowhere, the ceiling in my room caved in and water came pouring down! A worker on the second floor had busted a water pipe. Now it wasn't just flooding in Houston, it was also flooding in my room in Fiji! I quickly grabbed my belongings that were on the floor so they would not be ruined, and I called the front desk.

As the bellman helped me move to another room, he sensed my frustration. "Pastor Stringer, can I pray for you?"

I was a little surprised that he knew who I was.

"Yes, we all know you. When you preach at Pastor Suliasi's church we see you on television, and many of us have read your books," he said. He told me there are 20 believers working at the hotel, pastors and intercessors who make it their ministry to pray for and serve the guests who stay there. In their own quiet way, they are impacting the nations right where they are.

And this was not a unique situation. Throughout Fiji, you find so many people who truly love Jesus, with spirits so gentle and humble, who quietly yet proudly declare Christ as Lord. As they go about their work, you often hear them humming praise songs to Jesus.

The Father of all nations and all generations is taking them with this same message to the nations of the world.

Does this mean the country is completely free of all problems? No, not by any means. But God is definitely at work in their midst. He has honored the prayers of a handful of men and women who, years ago, cried out: "Lord, give us our nation!" And now, the Father of all nations and all generations is taking them with this same message to the nations of the world.

Every Nation, Every Ethnicity

When we say God will give us the nations, does this mean we believe every single nation will one day be a Christian nation? We can only answer that by looking at Scripture. One of the Greek words for "nation" is *ethnos*, as we see in Luke 21:10. From this term, we get our words "ethnic" and "ethnicity." I believe Scripture is revealing that one day people from every *nationality*, every *people group*, and every *ethnicity* will come to the revelation of Jesus as Lord.

I experienced a glimpse of this in September 2000 when Tom Hess hosted 1500 delegates in Jerusalem as part of the All Nations Convocation. From the top tower of our hotel, we could look down from one side and see Bethlehem, and we could look down from the other side and see the Old City of Jerusalem. It was a great vantage point for prayer, and all the intercessors took turns going up there to pray. We had believers with us who were Jewish, Arab, Persian, Japanese, Chinese, Korean, African, Hispanic, Latino—people from nearly every ethnicity who had come together to pray. It was a beautiful depiction of Micah 4, as we set aside our weapons of warfare and exchanged them for harvesting tools.

> *It was a beautiful depiction of Micah 4, as we set aside our weapons of warfare and exchanged them for harvesting tools.*

While we were there, the Intifada erupted. What a contrast to what was happening in the Convocation! There we were, laboring together through our commonality in Jesus Christ, and in the midst of it all this conflict breaks out between the Muslims and the Jews.

What was the difference? What was the reason for the contrast? As news reports every morning and every night painted a graphic picture of hatred between these people groups, why did our group, diverse as it was, experience no hatred toward one another? The *only* difference was this: Our group had a revelation of the love of Christ! We had a common bond in our relationship with Jesus.

When we come to the revelation of Jesus as the Prince of Peace, He gives us access to the Father, with open arms. We can then set aside our differences and reach a deeper level of relationship and intimacy with God and one another. Arabic and Jewish believers and other Christians can worship together because of the commonality that comes through a relationship with Jesus Christ. No one can deny the power of God's love when they witness the depth of relationship that exists among opposing groups — groups who cannot get along in the natural — when they come to the revelation of Jesus, His work on the cross, and the power of His resurrection.

Roots of Rejection

When the Intifada began, those of us at the Convocation began thinking about the conflict in relation to the reason we were there–to worship God — and we recognized the correlation. The surface issue is one of worship: Who will worship, who will be worshipped, and who will control the site of worship? Jews, Christians, and Muslims all recognize the Temple Mount as a significant or holy site. But the roots of the conflict go much deeper than that. It's a conflict that goes all the way back to Abraham, and the roots are embedded in woundedness and bitterness.

Abraham had one son (Ishmael) through Sarah's servant Hagar; one son (Isaac) through Sarah, his wife; and six sons through Keturah, the concubine he married after Sarah's death. In Genesis 21, Hagar and Ishmael are sent away to live in the desert, but God promised Hagar that from Ishmael would come a great nation. His descendants are the modern-day Arabs. Abraham also sent away the sons of Keturah. Historians say they settled in Persia (Iran) and Assyria, which includes the regions of modern-day Lebanon, Iraq, Iran, Syria, northern Jordan, and parts of western Afghanistan. Although God blessed all of Abraham's sons and provided for them, Isaac was the son of promise, the one who received Abraham's blessing and the inheritance of his covenant with God, according to biblical Scripture.

Isaac's son Esau—who was slightly older than his twin brother Jacob—married into the family of his uncle Ishmael (Genesis 28). It's interesting that both Ishmael and Esau were older brothers who did not receive the blessing normally reserved for the first-born son. So we see two slighted older brothers marrying into each other's lineage, resulting in a double portion of woundedness.

Could it be that when an individual carries deep-rooted wounds that they can be imparted to others around him, or even carried down for generations to come?

This raises an important question. Could it be that when an individual carries deep-rooted woundedness that it can be imparted to others around him, or even carried down for generations to come? Can the result be a corporate woundedness? It seems that what we still contend with today is a group of nations—the descendants of Ishmael, Esau (also known as Edom, whose descendants carried a deep animosity toward the Jews), and Keturah—wanting to make something happen by force because they did not receive their father's blessing.

Muslims, Jews, and Christians all have commonality in Father Abraham, who is a type of the Heavenly Father. Yet they are in conflict with one another! Regardless of our opinions of what is going on in the world from a political or even a religious point of view, we cannot deny that we have generations of brothers, cousins, and sons fighting amongst themselves. What began as roots of bitterness in individuals has been carried down from generation to generation to such an extent that is has even affected entire nations.

This is why it is so important for us to submit our hurts to the Father for healing and why we must learn to practice forgiveness.

When we operate out of wounded-ness and bitterness, we hinder our intimacy with others as well as our intimacy with God.

> *See to it that no one misses the grace of God and that no*
> *bitter root grows up to cause trouble and defile many*
> *-Hebrews 12:15*

Colossians 1:12 tells us we are to give *"thanks to the Father who has qualified us to be partakers of the inheritance of the saints in the light."*

No matter who we are or where we are from, God *Himself* qualifies us to receive His inheritance! He is the Father who wants to embrace us all, through the high cost of love He displayed through Christ and the work of the cross.

An Inheritance for All

Striving to take blessings by force is not exclusive to any single nation or religion. *Everyone* is looking for identity. *Everyone* wants a connection to the Creator. *Everyone* wants the love of a father. But it will not happen unless we put Jesus on the throne, for to know the Father we must first know the Son. We must exchange our wounded spirits and receive His Spirit of Adoption.

I don't want to bring the wounds from my past into my present relationships. I am empowered by Scripture to pull down every vain imagination. A love of truth helps me respond positively instead of reacting negatively to old insecurities, hurts, and pains.

A love of truth helps me respond positively instead of reacting negatively to old insecurities, hurts, and pains.

We can continue to react to wounds that have been passed down, even through the generations, or we can let the Son direct us to the open arms of the Heavenly Father, by which we are set free, healed, affirmed, approved, and accepted.

God wants all nations and all generations to know He has an inheritance for them. He wants to adopt us and to heal our lands, but we need His presence. That's what we've seen so beautifully in nations like Fiji, where people of different backgrounds have been able to reconcile through their commonality in Christ, in spite of any tension and conflict going on around them.

When we surrender to the sealing of the Spirit of Adoption and realize who Jesus is, God changes our hearts and enables us to touch the nations. Out of the wanderings of generations and the strivings of orphaned nations, the Heavenly Father wants to reveal Himself and pour out His blessings.

We must help the nations and generations to recognize by revelation that God has already given to us an awesome work of grace that entitles us to His whole inheritance.

He offers us an inheritance through His Son Jesus, and that inheritance *is* the nations of the world! From urban missions to un-reached people groups, from the inner city to foreign mission fields, from wherever we are now to the uttermost parts of the earth, God wants to give us the nations because He is the Father of all nations! And as we become His children through the Spirit of Adoption, the nations become our inheritance as well!

The church is God's tool and His answer to the despair in the nations of the world today. As never before, we see fatherless nations of spiritual orphans in search of identity. We see disasters, both human and natural. We see generations in the deserts of life, scattered, looking for a place of belonging and for a land to possess. We must help the nations and the generations recognize by revelation that God has already given to us an awesome work of grace that entitles us to His whole inheritance. We don't have to strive for it. We don't have to fight for it. We don't have to take it by force, according to the flesh. We take it by *promise* through His Son, Jesus!

The raging battles of our time are fought on our knees, for we wrestle not with flesh and blood. I love to quote Francis of Assisi, who said: "Preach the Gospel at all times. If necessary, use words." Let us make ourselves available to carry this message of good news to the nations, that they may know the richness of the blessings that await them through the Father of *all* nations and *all* generations!

10

The Spirit of Adoption

The Spirit of Adoption

I remember as a boy wanting so badly and so often to be with my father, but he wasn't there—so I would sit outside the house in the fort I built, just me and my little dog Bambi.

Dad was in the military, so that often took him away. He struggled with alcohol, so even when he was around, he wasn't really there. After he and my mother divorced, he was gone until I met him again in 1978, when I came to Houston to find him. My family was living in Washington state at the time, but I was restless, always trying to fill the void from something in my life that was missing. I felt like things would fall into place if I could just find my dad, so I contacted the military to find out where he was. He was living in Houston, and they let him know I was looking for him. Like this emerging generation in pursuit of spiritual fathers, I was in pursuit of my earthly father. It was a journey which ultimately led me to my Heavenly Father.

My dad had remarried when I found him, and he had a daughter, Judy. I was happy to see that his life had changed. But even so, it was hard for us to connect because of all the years that had passed. We really loved each other but neither of us knew how to express it or how to recover the intimacy that had been lost through the many years with no connection.

In 1990, I began to have a better understanding of my dad's life when I accompanied 17 veterans on a trip back to Viet Nam for healing. For 15 years, these men—though they were Christians— had struggled with various issues, such as nightmares, drugs, and alcohol. They had problems in their marriages. They suffered "survivors guilt," having watched their friends die right before their eyes.

As we approached our destination and the plane began its descent, you could have heard a pin drop. I watched these men as they looked out the windows of the plane, and tears were streaming down their faces. Over the next few days, as I listened and observed and saw the pain in their lives, I began to understand why my own father and stepfather—who had both served in Viet Nam—didn't know how to engage with me as a son and why they, too, had turned to alcohol to cover up the memories and the atrocities of the war. It caused me to love them even more and gave me the heart of God to see them saved, healed, and delivered.

In 1993, I was away on a ministry trip when I got word that my dad had been diagnosed with military-related lung cancer. At that time he began to reach out to me, trying to re-connect. He wanted to talk to his son Doug. He would say things like, "Remember the time we did this" and "Remember the time we did that." I realized there were so many memories I had stuffed because all I could recall were the times he wasn't there. He wanted to bring back the past we had lost, but I didn't know how to receive from him or how to reach out to him.

By that time, Dad had not been drinking or smoking for 10 years. His wife, Margaret, had noticed he was reading his Bible in the mornings. Once when I was traveling, I asked a pastor friend to visit him for me. Afterward, he told me my dad had been listening to the Bible on tape for over a year. He had read my books and was listening to my teaching tapes. The pastor assured me my dad had a relationship with Jesus.

The entire time he was sick, my dad never complained. As his illness progressed, I would call him to see how he was doing, and the answer was always the same: "I'm fine, things are great!" I always promised him I would go see him whenever I got back from my next trip, but it never happened.

Then Margaret started calling me to say, "Doug, you really need to go see him. He's not doing well." For a whole week, I planned to see him, but things kept coming up. It was finally Friday, and I was doing a two-hour program at a local radio station. I had every intention of seeing him as soon as I was finished, but in the middle of the show I got a "911" message on my beeper. It was Cynthia from the office trying to reach me.

"Doug, I don't know how to tell you this," she said when I called, "but your dad has passed away."

All week, the Holy Spirit had been nudging me, "Go see your father. Go see your father." But I was too busy—doing "God's work." The doctors had told us he had six months to live, but it was only 90 days later and he was gone. I remember sitting on the couch in that radio station trying to deal with all my emotions. I didn't know what to say or what to do. I kept hearing one song playing over and over in my head, "Cats in the Cradle" by Harry Chapin. The song speaks first of a little boy who wants to be with his dad, but his dad never has time for him. When the dad grows older, the tables are turned. Now the dad wants to be with his son, but the son has his own life. There's no time for dad. At that moment, I realized how that happened in my own life, and how much I regretted that past week of missed opportunities.

We live lives full of missed opportunities. How many times do we put aside those we love because we're too busy for them? We're too busy to tell our parents, our children, our husbands, and our wives: "I love you."

How many times do we walk out the door frustrated with the ones we love? We have no certainty we will see that person again—we have no guarantees about tomorrow. We must cherish what we have and take advantage of the moments with the people God has placed in our lives.

And how many times do we neglect our Heavenly Father, our Abba, who wants so much to seal us with His Spirit of Adoption, to place us as His children in His family? How often do we forget that He wants to give us a new name in life, a new position in life? He is the one who has gone to such great lengths to bring us into His family, yet how much we neglect Him.

For God so loved the world that He gave His only begotten Son, that whoever believes in Him should not perish but have everlasting life.

-John 3:16

We go about our lives wanting Him to be our "sugar daddy" instead of our Abba-Father, the one whose lap we can crawl onto as we tell Him our struggles and the difficulties we're going through. "Oh, Father! I need Your wisdom. I need Your love. I need Your direction. I'm lonely today. I'm hurting today. Would you just hold on to me and speak to me?"

He wants that from us so much! He wants it so much that He gave His only begotten Son so we could be sealed by the Spirit of Adoption and placed as sons and daughters in His family. Let's not miss out on opportunities with our friends and our families, and let's especially not neglect so great a salvation, so great a love from our Father.

For God so loved the world…

God desires His best for us: a revelation of the Father, the identity of the Father, the embrace of the Father. That really is what the Spirit of Adoption is all about. And it comes with a promise — it comes with joint heir-ship with His Son Jesus Christ, because in Him we, too, are the children of God.

> *God desires His best for us: a revelation of the Father, the identity of the Father, the embrace of the Father.*

Yes, I was a boy who so badly wanted a father. But my Heavenly Father was there for me — He is there for all of us. And now He can help us be good fathers and mothers to a generation in pursuit of spiritual fathers and spiritual mothers. We don't know how to do it, but He can give us the grace. He can teach us how to parent this emerging, orphaned, fatherless generation that needs direction. He can teach us how to be their covering and how to introduce them to their Heavenly Father through the Spirit of Adoption.

A New Name

When Jack Hayford's mother went to be with the Lord, he spoke of the inheritance he and his brother Jim received after her home-going. "It wasn't that we were worthy in ourselves to receive the inheritance, but only because we carried the name 'Hayford.' We automatically received an inheritance because of the name."

Because we've been purchased by the blood of Jesus and because we have a new God-given name, we now have an inheritance. This is not because of our good works or because we've earned it, but because we are sealed by His name.

Ephesians 1:13 says, *"In Him you, also, trusted after you heard the Word of Truth, the gospel of your salvation, in whom also, having believed you were sealed, with the Holy Spirit of Promise."*

The Spirit of Adoption is really the Spirit of Promise—the promise of a new life. If we are His children, then we are *"heirs of God and joint heirs with Christ. If indeed we suffer with Him then we may, also, be glorified together"* (Romans 8:17). At the root of the Hebrew word used here for "suffer" (*sumpascho*) is the word for "passion" (*pascho*). If we have fellowship in His sufferings, then we have the passion of Christ in us and a heart to do His will.

> ### *The Spirit of Adoption is really the Spirit of Promise - the promise of a new life.*

Because we share as heirs with Jesus, we are qualified to assume God the Father's divine power and nature.

"Even to them I will give in My house and within My walls a place and a name better than that of sons and daughters; I will give them an everlasting name that shall not be cut off."

-Isaiah 56:5

The old ways of sin and death are overtaken with Christ's life, which moves us into a position of adoption, a place of promise. He gives us a new life, a new name, and a new status in life, then seals us by the Spirit.

Placed as Sons

The term "adoption" implies the act of officially taking the child of another to be one's own. The finished work of the cross, through grace, is how we come to this. The Spirit certifies the son-ship.

For as many as are led by the Spirit of God, these are the sons of God. For you did not receive the Spirit of Bondage

> *again to fear, but you received the Spirit of Adoption by*
> *whom we cry out "Abba! Father!"*
>
> *-Romans 8:14-15*

The Aramaic here is "Abba," which we already know can be translated "Daddy" or "Papa." Imagine crawling into your father's lap and saying, "Hey, Papa" or "Hey, Daddy" or "Hey, Abba."

God is bringing us into this place of adoption by which we can call Him "Abba." It's no longer God out in the cosmic universe and you and me down here as specks of sand on the earth. He knows us by name. He knew us when we were in our mothers' wombs. He wants to have an intimate relationship with us. He wants us to call Him "Abba."

Jesus used that same term in the Garden of Gethsemane, when He cried, "Abba!" Likewise, in each and every one of our lives—no matter what struggles, fears, or insecurities we encounter—we can come boldly before the Lord, like a child comes to his Papa when the Spirit of Adoption has sealed, verified, and certified that we are truly children of the living God.

Literally translated, "adoption" means "placing as a son." It means that we are now placed as genuine sons—we are part of the bloodline! We have been placed as sons or daughters in the family of God. We are not merely just adopted on paper, we also carry His name.

> *But seek first the kingdom of God and His righteousness*
> *and **all** these things shall be added unto you*
> *-Matthew 6:33 [emphasis added]*

We not only have the promise of inheritance, we also get *all* the benefits of being in God's family. Our new names are not only written in the Lamb's Book of Life, but we are also given the promise of inheritance and the benefits of the Kingdom. It's a legal placement in the family of God, a new positioning, a new identity with a promise.

We give thanks to God for our inheritance.

Restoring Broken Trust

My mom, dad, and step-dad are all with Jesus now, and I praise the Lord that they all came to salvation before their home-goings. But growing up was difficult.

I was nine when my father and mother divorced. My mother remarried, and my stepfather was an atheist. We got along really well when he wasn't drinking. But because of the alcohol, I never knew how he was going to react in any given situation. I was already dealing with my own hurts stemming from the separation from my father, so I put up walls and sometimes reacted in rebellion.

What I didn't understand then was that my father and stepfather both had hurts and issues of their own that I could not see until I was grown. My dad had lost a teen-age daughter from his first marriage when she died in a car accident on her first date. My stepfather had no relationship with his biological father, who had been in prison, although his own stepfather loved him as a son. They both had issues from being involved in the Viet Nam war, and my dad had also served in the war in Korea. But as a child, I could not understand all these things.

This is not meant to excuse or justify the actions of people when they are abusive or alcoholics, but sometimes even as adults and as Christians we find it easy to criticize those who are in authority — our parents, our spiritual coverings, and our pastors. We have such high expectations of them. We don't see that they, too, have a window of their souls. Just like us, they have issues to work through, and that can only happen for any of us through a connection with our Heavenly Father.

When we have had bad experiences with our fathers, we

often have trouble receiving God as Father. We have difficulty trusting Him. We must break away from the fears of earthly situations into an understanding that we can trust God. He knows exactly what our needs are, and He will never leave us nor forsake us.

"I'll Be Your Father"

When I became a Christian, Dr. Ed Cole became a spiritual father to me. In 1989, he invited me to attend a men's event with himself and Ben Kinchlow. It was a large father-son gathering at a church in Dallas.

Dr. Cole called me and said, "Doug, I just want to make sure you're coming to Dallas for the men's event."

"No sir, I won't be coming," I said. I was going through some difficult situations, and I just didn't feel like being around people. But Dr. Cole persisted.

"Doug, you really need to be here."

Finally, I relented, and I honored Dr. Cole by going to the event.

As I boarded the plane, I hadn't eaten in over two weeks—not because I was fasting by choice, but because I had been forced into a fast by the Spirit. I was grieving in my heart about a lot of things. And now I was on my way to this event for fathers and sons, but I never felt like I had a father. Even as a Christian, I had come to know Jesus but not the Father's heart and the Father's love. I understood the cross. I understood grace. But I still didn't understand the Spirit of Adoption or intimacy with the Father. Because of my upbringing, it was difficult to understand the revelation of "Abba."

During the event, Dr. Cole issued an invitation to come to the altar. Hundreds of men were there—fathers and their sons—and I watched them running to the altar, embracing, forgiving,

"Doug," I heard God say in His still small voice, "I'm your Father. I want to do things with you that you never did with a father."

~~~

and repenting. Tears of joy began to stream down my face for that emerging generation and their fathers, but mingled with them were tears of sadness and a longing for the love and companionship of a father that I had never understood. I had done special things occasionally with my father and stepfather, but it was never consistent. I had never learned to snow ski. I had never learned to swim. I had never been deep sea fishing. Here I was, already in my 30s, and there was a whole list of things I had never done, the normal things sons and fathers do together.

"Doug," I heard God say in His still small voice, "I'm your Father. I want to do things with you that you never did with a father."

My response was somewhat skeptical. I couldn't comprehend how I could have that kind of companionship with someone who wasn't human, who wasn't tangible. Besides, how could I, as an adult, go back to being a child?

A year later, I was on the ski slopes of Crested Butte, Colorado. I took the "Never Ever" class and watched seven-year-olds zip past me with no poles. I thought skiing was the stupidest sport I had ever been a part of. But, finally, after a couple of days, I was actually skiing one of the slopes. And though I was still falling a lot, it didn't matter anymore. At one point, I stopped and looked at the beauty of God's creation.

Suddenly the Lord spoke to me, reminding me of His promise and all the things we had done together throughout that year. I had gone deep sea fishing for the first time in my life with pastor friends in Australia, and I caught the biggest fish of the entire group—it was huge! I called it "Jaws." None of the other pastors had caught anything that size the entire summer. I had played golf for the first time in Australia, too, and I hit the same kangaroo twice! My staff jokes that every time I go to Australia now the kangaroos put on their crash helmets. During that same year, I went to a lake, jumped off a boat, and went water skiing for the first time. I never did get up, so it was more like "knee boarding" (of course, "knee time" is the best posture for me anyway.) But I did it! Me and my Father, me and my "Abba." And now, here I was snow skiing in the Rocky Mountains!

As I looked back on that year and all the things I did for the first time, I realized my Heavenly Father had become my Abba-Father. He had kept His promise and had become tangible to me by the Spirit of Adoption.

Learning to be Sons

It took me years, even as a Christian, to come to the revelation that my Father in Heaven has an inheritance for me. I could believe for everyone else. I could pray and agree and see God do miracles for others, but not for me. An inheritance is passed from father to son, and I didn't even know how to be a son. But when we look in Scripture, we can see examples of good sons and bad sons, both in the spiritual and in the natural.

Elisha was a son to Elijah, and he received a double portion of his anointing because he honored Elijah. Gehazi, Elisha's servant, could have been a son, too, but instead he chose to dishonor Elisha when he asked for a reward from the servant of Naaman (2 Kings 5). He was stricken with leprosy because of his unfaithfulness.

Elisha was persistent and stayed with Elijah, not because he wanted an inheritance of monetary value or even because he wanted a double portion of Elijah's anointing. He sought after the prophet because he wanted to be with him as he lived his everyday life in God. He knew that being in the presence of the prophet was priceless. He stayed with his mentor until his death because he dearly loved him, not because of some future benefit that could only be realized through witnessing Elijah's death.

Earlier I shared thoughts from Pastor Mike regarding the marks of a father. A son, he adds, is someone who stays, who doesn't leave just because he is corrected. A son does not operate in the flesh, he is led by the Spirit (Romans 8:14). He cares about his father's work and about his father's ministry, unlike Hophni and Phineas, who destroyed the ministry of their father, Eli the priest.

A son recognizes the value just of being in His Father's presence.

I was invited to sit in on a roundtable of leaders of the emerging generations, hosted by Mission America in New York City. "To have spiritual fathers in the room brought everything up to a greater level," said one of our hosts. "Their presence and spoken words of exhortation challenged the group and kept things connected through another perspective."

A son recognizes the value just of being in his father's presence.

He Was There All Along

I used to lament the fact I had missed out on so many father-son opportunities with my earthly father and stepfather. But after God adopted me, I realized my Heavenly Father was with me all along.

God wants to be a Father to the fatherless, to adopt them in these fatherless days. He wants to nurture us and care for us, to give us His nature and power, yet He also is a Father who chastises and disciplines His children. Some of you may experience lives of chaos because you never had a father to show discipline. But God desires to offer you His discipline, and in His discipline there is peace. God's discipline is a good thing.

Quite simply, God wants to adopt us, to take ownership of us, to make us one of His children. He wants to give us His inheritance, His love, even His discipline. He wants us to take on His name, His legacy, His lineage. He wants to take care of us and nurture us in ways far greater than any earthly parent ever could. He desperately wants to be a Father to the fatherless, to seal us into His family by the Spirit of Adoption.

Part IV

That's My Girl! That's My Boy!

11

Honor and Blessing

Honor and Blessing

Growing up, I longed for the acceptance, approval, and affirmation of a father. I can remember being at baseball games and wanting so badly for my step-dad to tell me he was proud of me. Instead, as he tried to cover up the pains in his own life with alcohol, he would often come to my games drinking. Rather than affirming me, he would say things that embarrassed me. As an adult, I was able to lead him to Christ and our relationship was healed as I saw his life through the eyes of God. But as a boy, the absence of affirmation was a painful thing to endure. Even now as a grown man trying to be a spiritual father to others, I still find myself at times longing to be affirmed and acknowledged by father figures.

Likewise, this emerging generation is looking for someone to whom they can pour out their hearts with the joys and challenges of serving the Kingdom of God. They need guidance, counsel, and direction. They need someone they can go to and say, "Daddy, how did I do?" Like all of us, they need to hear someone say, "That's my girl! That's my boy!"

Even Jesus received verbal affirmation from His Father. When He was baptized in the Jordan River by John the Baptist, a voice came from heaven saying, *"This is My beloved Son, in whom I am well pleased." (Matthew 3:17)* That was God the Creator, the Father of heaven and earth, giving complete approval and affirmation of His Son before the people.

Likewise, he is saying to those of us in Christ, "That's my boy! That's my girl!" Oh, to hear those words from a father!

God knows our needs, and He knows when we are lacking these things from our earthly fathers. He longs for us to come to Him at those times, saying "Did I do good? Are you proud of me?" He loves saying to us, "Well done!"

But how can we know we are pleasing to God? How can we be sure we are walking in ways that are making Him proud?

God's love for us is unconditional; it is not something we earn. We are His sons and daughters if we have been sealed by the Spirit of Adoption. But there are principles we can apply to our lives and attributes we can practice that are attractive to God. Though others are listed throughout Scripture, I often teach on four of these attributes: holiness, humility, honesty, and honor.

Holiness is not a religious, external formula or legalistic piety, but submission and surrender of the heart to the Creator of the universe who so loved us that He gave His only son for us. Holiness is our response as an act of worship, an act of love. It is not an external show or facade, but an attitude of the heart.

God wants us to walk in *humility*, yet to be confident in who we are in Him. Humility precedes exaltation.

> *Therefore humble yourselves under the mighty hand of God, that He may exalt you in due time.*
>
> *-I Peter 5:6*

God wants us to be people of *honesty* so that we can discern between the Spirit of Truth and the Spirit of Error (I John 4:4-6). Scripture makes it clear, dishonesty is not attractive to God.

Lying lips are an abomination to the Lord, But those who deal truthfully are His delight.

-Proverbs 12:22

Finally, God is attracted to those who practice *honor*. Honor releases blessing. Malachi 1:6 says we are to honor God because He is our Father. Exodus 20:12 tells us to honor our parents so we will have long life. And when it comes to releasing a multi-generational anointing, honor is key.

Honoring the Former

Jesus epitomized *honor*. While men reached for thrones to build their own kingdoms, Jesus reached for a towel to wash men's feet. Just as God is calling the older generations to believe in, inspire, and empower the younger, He is calling the younger to honor the older. In God's plan, honor releases blessing.

> *When it comes to releasing a multi-generational anointing, honor is key.*

In 2001, our ministry honored several key leaders in the city with the Golden Towel awards, given to individuals who had been tangible expressions of Christ. One of the recipients was Dodie Osteen, widow of the late John Osteen of Houston's Lakewood Church. When I was young and new in the ministry, Brother Osteen and Dodie were an encouragement to me personally and always made me feel welcome. Dodie even tells people now that she thinks of me as a son. I wanted, in this small way, to express my honor to her not only for the inspiration she and Brother Osteen were to me but to recognize all they had done for so many others as well.

A few years later, in 2005, the River Oaks Chapter of Women's Aglow in Houston invited me to speak at their annual Christmas banquet. I serve on their advisory board, but I did not know they were planning to honor me that day for my service to them and for being, in their eyes, a father to the city. Dodie was asked to introduce me and to present the gifts they had selected for me: a beautiful, small treasure chest filled with the same gems that are on the Levitical ephod and a white linen towel, signifying the servanthood of Christ. Because I have trouble seeing myself as a spiritual father, I was humbled that these ladies—especially Dodie, a spiritual mother in our city—would honor me that way. Years earlier, we had chosen to honor her, and now she was blessing me.

The older generations have an inheritance to pass to the younger, but inheritance is received, not taken. The younger must be willing to honor the older truly to receive the inheritance.

A few days earlier, I had been honored in a similar fashion by Jose and Magda Hermida. Magda ministers to the Hispanic community not only in Houston but through her radio program heard throughout South America. They invited me to speak at their annual Christmas breakfast, with an audience of over 1000 ladies and ministry leaders. Before I spoke, they honored me with a plaque that reads, "We honor you as a father, covering, and inspiration, not only to us but to those you encounter wherever you go. We love you and appreciate your love and concern for us all."

Because Jose and Magda choose to honor me as a father—though they are several years older than I and are considered a father and mother themselves to so many people—I desire to bless them. I am committed to letting them share in my inheritance by supporting their ministry any way I can.

Other ministries in Houston honor us for paving the path for their ministries. Some work in the inner city areas where we first began our own ministry. Because they honor us, we bless them and invest in them by providing our time, our facilities, and our resources.

When you honor a person, you are endeared to him or her, and he or she wants to bless you in return. The older generations have an inheritance to pass to the younger, but inheritance is received, not taken. The younger must be willing to honor the older to receive the inheritance.

During one of our Compassion Coalition/Pastors and Leaders meetings, we honored three fathers in our city who had each been serving in ministry for over 50 years. They were Bishop Kossie, from Latter-Day Deliverance Revival Church in Houston's inner city; Pastor Cantu, who leads El Tabernaculo, a Hispanic church; and Pastor Karmout from the Arab Evangelical Church.

The audience included over 100 pastors and leaders from all denominations and types of ministries. During an extended ministry time at the end of the meeting, each person had the opportunity to receive a spiritual father's blessing in prayer from each of these leaders. As I looked across the room, I was impressed with the genuine diversity and the beauty of the dynamics of the day as we witnessed a multi-generational and multi-ethnic honoring of these spiritual fathers who are all finishing their races well. As we lingered in the presence of God, His anointing was so powerful and so evident many would comment on it afterward. Pastor and Mrs. Karmout even said it reminded them of the revival in Jerusalem in the 1970s. Because we honored those who have gone before us, God chose to bless our time together.

A generation that recognizes the importance of honoring the former and does so will create in the former a desire to release blessing upon them in return, which will result in a corporate multi-generational anointing.

"Come With Us"

Many in the emerging generation recognize they need the wisdom and experience of a former generation. They may have a different way of presentation, a different style of music — a different style of *everything* — but they know they can't completely disregard the ways of the former generation. The only way to cross over into the promised land of blessing and destiny is to recognize and honor the former and say, "Give us your blessing *and* join with us."

2 Kings 6 reports how the sons of the prophets came to Elisha, the older prophet who had received a double portion from his spiritual father, Elijah. The place they lived was not big enough, and they asked for his blessing and his permission to build elsewhere. To me, this is an analogy of a generation coming to say, "What we're doing is unique, and what we desire to do is different. But we recognize we need your blessing."

Elisha gave them his blessing, then they asked for more — they asked him to accompany them on their journey. There is no mention of him actually doing the work, but he was present. The younger prophets didn't *need* him to do the work because they knew what to do. The same is true in the emerging generation. They are full of vision as a prophetic generation. They will fulfill the dreams of the previous generations. But if they recognize they need the wisdom and covering of those who have gone before, they will be unstoppable! Because Elisha went along, the sons of the prophets felt strengthened just by his presence.

Later, when they lost their axe-head — which represents their passion, edge, direction, and strength — they went to Elisha for wisdom. Quite simply, he told them, "Take me back to where you lost it." Likewise today, those who have been around a while and have experienced the hard times of ministry can help others rediscover their passion and zeal. They can help them return to their first love.

How does this happen? By directing those who are discouraged by life to go back to where they lost their passion and zeal—where they were disappointed, where they were disillusioned by leaders, where they turned their focus from God to man—we can walk them through the simple act of finding it again. Anything that is lost can only be found where you lost it.

The former has to bless the emerging and the emerging has to honor the former. All of us working together can accomplish mighty exploits for God.

We've seen the former rain. We've glimpsed the latter rain. But when the former and latter rains come together, the result is an open floodgate releasing the rivers of God.

The Principle at Work in My Own Life

In the early 1980s, when I was introduced to the ministry of Dr. Ed Cole, his message of consecration gripped my heart and connected with my spirit. In 1983, I began serving his ministry as a volunteer in a temporary Houston office that was the headquarters for a Christian men's event scheduled for April of the following year.

When a Christian businessman who had befriended me invited me to join him at a meeting so I could meet Dr. Cole, I was hesitant, but decided to go anyway. I respected Dr. Cole's position and did not want to pursue him. But in the middle of the meeting, Dr. Cole pulled me aside so he could speak to me. He said he had heard about my work and asked how much it would cost him to hire me to be the National Young Adult Coordinator for the 1984 event.

"Dr. Cole, I'm not a hireling," I said. "I'm already serving you full-time and I will continue to do so because I believe in your message. I appreciate the offer, but God is my source, and I feel like the Lord has given me a challenge to serve you for this event because of its significance and the impact it will have on the men in our nation."

I served Dr. Cole not only for that event but for years to come, and he became like a spiritual father to me. I didn't pursue him for what he could do for me, but God validated me through him as he invested in me, not just with time, but also in character. I didn't necessarily spend a lot of time with him, but what time I did spend with him was quality.

As years went by, people would tell me the kind things Dr. Cole said about me. I realized I was receiving an inheritance from him, not because I asked for one, but because I served him in *honor*. Honor released blessing. Once Dr. Cole was ministering in another country, and someone there told him how I quoted him all the time. He responded by saying I didn't have to quote him, because all the things he taught me were mine now. What I learned from Dr. Cole became my inheritance, part of my DNA.

When my real father and stepfather died, they both left me golf clubs — and I don't even golf! But When Dr. Cole died, I received something very valuable. When he first started out in ministry, he prayed in an old church late at night to prepare for the next day's service. He would put a blanket over his shoulders to keep himself warm. Often, his kids would sleep on the pews next to him while he prayed so they could be close to him, and he put blankets on them as well. When his ministry grew and he began traveling, he would take the bedspread from the hotel room and put it over his shoulders before he prayed. It was a habit that had become part of his prayer life. Years ago, someone made him a handmade prayer blanket. I can imagine the hundreds or even thousands of tears that were shed and the countless of hours of prayer that took place under that blanket, and when he died he left it to me. Because of the honor I gave him over the years, he wanted to bless me. It is a gift I treasure because it represents the greater inheritance of what Dr. Cole's life was all about. It is a reminder to me of all the times I heard him pray, even when he was physically exhausted from ministering, "God, give me a little more time to reach a few more men, a few more families." What I received from serving Dr. Cole is an inheritance that will take me far beyond riches of gold or silver.

I was also blessed to have a relationship with another mighty man of God, Leonard Ravenhill. I didn't pursue him either, we just happened to connect. He had come across a pre-published book I wrote in 1990 and began to peruse it. Something about the book engaged his heart, and he began writing notes to me and praying for me. Eventually I got to meet him and to visit with him from time to time. I came to think of him as a spiritual grandfather. Sometimes I would feel impressed to call him, and he would say, "Oh, dear Brother Doug...I was just praying for you." I was so humbled that someone so important in the Kingdom of God would take time to pray for me.

What I received from serving Dr. Cole is an inheritance that will take me far beyond riches of gold or silver.

Before Brother Ravenhill died, he was in a semi-coma. One day I called his wife, Martha, to see how he was doing. She began telling me how people from all over the world were coming to see him, and some of them would actually take his hand and place it on their forehead, expecting to get a double portion of his anointing. In the same manner, I sometimes have people who try to coerce me into being a spiritual father to them in attempts to receive a blessing. But relationship does not work that way, and inheritance does not work that way. Inheritance cannot be taken, it is earned by imbibing the character and spirit of the message and the messenger. You can't just take it, it is a mutual gift.

I was in an airport when I got the call from Susie at my office that Brother Ravenhill had passed away, so I immediately rerouted my flight to attend his funeral. On the way there, I was contemplating his life and the many people with whom he had relationship—people like David Wilkerson, the late Keith Green, and Jacob Aranza. Suddenly, I doubted my own relationship with him. A voice in my head seemed to say, *Who do you think you are to think that he is really your spiritual grandfather? Yes, you did spend time with him and you had a relationship with him, but he was such an important man. Did he really see you that way?*

I attended the funeral, then went to the burial. Here was this great man of God being buried in an obscure cemetery outside a small rural town in East Texas. It so typified the humility of his life. While I was there, God Himself began dispelling the doubts I had about my relationship with him as various people came up to me and asked, "Are you Doug Stringer?" They began telling me how Brother Ravenhill always spoke so highly of me and how he recommended my book to them.

Suddenly, it didn't matter how much time I'd spent with him. What mattered was that, without even trying, I had received a rich inheritance from him in the spirit. Because I had honored him, he had blessed me. Even now, as we are completing the manuscript of this book, I've been asked to endorse a book written by his son David, who carries on his father's passion for prayer, worship, and living holy for God. So I not only gained an inheritance of blessing in the spirit, I also gained the blessing of friendship with his son.

A Lost Art

In many cultures of the world, honor is still practiced, especially in the form of honoring previous generations. It is not considered unusual for parents or grandparents to be cared for in their latter years in the homes of the younger generation. Instead of seeing the elderly as a burden, they are viewed as a blessing, a vast resource of wisdom and knowledge. Even in America, there once was a time when we took pains to honor the elderly, recognizing them for their faithfulness and wisdom. The younger generations appreciated the experience and insights of their elders.

I was reminded of my own heritage of honor when I watched

the movie *The Last Samurai*. The Japanese word *samurai* simply means "servant." The entire duty of the samurai was to serve the emperor and defend his honor.

After my mother became a widow, my sister and brother both asked her to live with them. But my mother wouldn't have it. "I live with my oldest boy, Dougie!" I was 38 years old, single, and leading an international ministry — buying a house with my mother was not exactly the path I had envisioned for my life at that time! But as the oldest Asian son, I knew it was my responsibility to care for her. In 1996, she moved in with me and lived with me for nearly eight years until she moved to Austin to be near my sister. She had begun having some health problems, and I was traveling a lot. A year and a half later, she went to be with Jesus, just a few weeks after she was diagnosed with cancer. Now, I wouldn't trade those eight years we had together for anything in the world. I am so thankful I chose to honor her that way.

I still find myself honoring my mother by obeying certain things she taught me, like taking off my shoes before going into the house. Anytime I determine to walk through the house fully shod, I can only get so far before I hear her voice saying, "Dougie! Do you have your shoes on? Douglas, take off your shoes!" Now I even make my guests take off their shoes!

I also remember my mother telling me not to throw tissues in the toilet. "Dougie, they clog the drain!" I would argue with her that there was no difference in tissues and toilet paper. Years later, I learned she was right when I saw it on television. It was confirmed again by a woman who heard me tell the story when I was preaching at a church in Cheshire, Connecticut. She sent me an email entitled, "Your mother was right":

> *I heard you tell the story about your mother and her opposi-tion to having tissues thrown into the toilet. She was right, you know! I laughed to myself as I thought what my 9 year old would tell you if you were to walk up and ask him why we*

don't throw tissues into the toilet. A couple of years ago Chaska and I set up a small experiment. We put a tissue in a cup of water and toilet paper in another cup of water and let it sit overnight. Sure enough, the next day the toilet paper had broken up very well and the tissue was still completely intact. While I was talking with my husband about what you had said, I looked at Chaska and asked, "Chaska, why don't we throw tissues into the toilet?" He looked up at me over the rim of his glasses and said, "Because they'll clog the drain." Then, knowing that our six-year-old is trained not to throw the tissues into the toilet but

We have neither learned nor passed on the principles of honor in our homes, much less our schools or workplaces.

wondering if he understands why, I asked, "Kenya, why don't we throw tissues into the toilet?" He raised his curly mop and said, "Because we frow dem in the trash." "But, Kenya, why do we throw them in the trash?" "Because we can't frow dem in the toiwet." "Kenya, what would happen if we threw them in the toilet?" He raised his curly mop again and paused for a moment. Then, making a gagging noise and sticking out his precious little tongue, he said, "It would choke!"

Honor Guards for God

Unfortunately, it seems this type of honor for the previous generation is becoming a lost art. We have neither learned nor passed on the principles of honor in our homes, much less our schools or workplaces. And if we did not learn to honor our parents—largely because our parents were absent—how will we learn to honor our God?

Our ministry hosted a meeting for our Disaster Response and Preparedness Network in Washington D.C. with ministry leaders from around the nation with whom we had partnered during relief efforts for Hurricanes Katrina and Rita. One of our guests, Pastor

Burchett from Kirbyville, Texas, and Somebody Cares Jasper/
Newton Counties, spent some of his free time visiting Arlington
Cemetery. He had previously preached a sermon based on the
changing of the guards at the Tomb of the Unknown Soldier and
now, watching it in person, was deeply impacted by the display of
honor. According to Pastor Burchett:

> *"The tomb is guarded 24-hours-per-day and 365-days-per
> year by specially trained members of the 3rd United States
> Infantry. This select group of sentinels is called the 'Honor
> Guard'. . . Being selected to stand watch over the graves of
> the Unknown Soldiers is one of the highest honors a soldier
> in the United States Army can be granted.*
>
> *". . . day or night, and regardless of the elements, the tomb
> is guarded, and has been guarded, every minute of every
> day since 1937. The sentinels never allow any feeling of
> cold or heat to be seen by anyone and they never change the
> way they guard the tomb, even at night when there is no one
> watching. The sentinels do what they do for the ones they
> are honoring, not for spectators or for their own personal
> advancement. They genuinely believe that the Unknown
> Soldiers deserve the very best they have to give."*

Pastor Burchett challenges us to apply the honor guard's
dedication to our own dedication to God the Father.

> *"Twenty-four hours a day and 365 days a year, the Lord
> God Almighty sits in the center of heaven. He invites
> men and women to receive the highest of all honors in
> the Kingdom of God, that of coming into His Presence
> to minister to Him. The disciplines of holiness and honor
> require wholeheartedness, dignity, perseverance, diligence,
> praise, humility, reverence, respect, and vigilance. Without
> these characteristics, no one can stand before and minister
> to the Lord."*

Honor releases blessing. First, we are to honor God. We are to honor His Word, His Person, and His Character so we can walk in His blessing and favor. We honor Him by practicing godly characteristics and principles, and by exhibiting the character of Christ. We honor Him by giving our time and resources.

Second, we are to honor our parents. Even though we may not always agree with them, we disagree while maintaining respect and honor. Honoring our parents is the first commandment to come with a promise, the blessing of long life.

Third, we are told to honor spiritual authorities God has placed in our lives. Again, even if we don't agree with them, we must still respect their office and the fact that God has appointed them. We remember that they are human and flawed, but we serve as unto God, and therefore, we honor them.

Fourth, we honor one another: spouses, family, friends, and co-workers.

And last, we are to honor former generations. It would benefit us greatly to study the origins of some of our favorite hymns and to read about the spiritual giants who have gone before us, those sold-out pioneers in the faith who paved the way for our ministries upon the earth.

Wisdom doesn't come solely from our successes, but also from our failures. The wisdom of the elders was often obtained by them as they learned from their mistakes. Honoring those who have gone before us can save us from experiencing the same problems they did. It can be liberating for us.

As we honor God, our parents (in the natural and the spiritual), our authorities, those who have gone before us, and one another, we position ourselves to hear those wonderful words from our Father: "Well done! That's my girl! That's my boy!"

12

*Raising a Standard
of Righteousness*

Raising a Standard of Righteousness

In 2004, I was invited on a ministry trip to Brazil, a country with more than 186 million people. I was told that 12 million of them are homeless teenagers and children, and, according to various census records, one third of the population lives in poverty.

While there, I was asked to speak to a group of youth leaders. I arrived to find the place packed with several thousand young people and their leaders, filling all the seats in the church and standing outside. I was moved by the energy and excitement of this generation and to see such hunger and passion in the midst of despair. The very facet of Brazilian society that is under oppression is the one that is rising up and setting the standard!

All over the world, God is calling forth a generation endued with power to

All over the world, God is calling forth a generation endued with power to raise a standard of passion, purity and purpose.

181

raise a standard of passion, purity, and purpose. They are young people who are not looking at the circumstances. Instead, they look at the promises of God and say, "In the midst of impossibility, we see a God of possibility."

We're witnessing the "de-CHRIST-ing" of a generation. As a nation, we've lowered the standard, and it's time for every generation to raise that standard once again.

In one country that is known as a Christian country, a pastor was arrested for speaking out on moral issues, including homosexuality, while teaching from Romans 1. And in another nation where I go to preach, those who oppose the Gospel are trying to have legislation changed to be more antagonistic toward the church. This is becoming increasingly true in America as well. We have free speech unless it goes against the counter-cultures who contradict the mores of our society.

What have we come to? We're witnessing the "de-CHRIST-ing" of a generation. As a nation, we've lowered the standard, and it's time for every generation to raise that standard once again and say, "We will not be moved because we're going to fight a battle, and we're willing to die for it."

Many voices of compromise are out there, but the Bible is our standard for truth. We must set up His Word as our own standard, raise it, and follow after God with our whole hearts.

What Is A Standard?

Historically, a standard serves three purposes:

- To identify a group (tribal or national)
- To claim possession of a space or territory
- For festivity or celebration

Each of the 12 tribes of Israel had a standard or flag identifying its tribe, in camp and in battle. In battle, a standard is used to identify the regiment or platoon and to communicate a variety of messages, including nationality and instructions to advance or retreat.

A standard is also a banner, and God's banner over us is love. Jesus has already set a standard over us and is calling us to raise that same standard of life, love, and purpose for others to follow when the world is getting dark. It's a standard of hope! A generation who raises the standard of God and does not diminish or lower it will impact the rest of their generation to follow.

God is calling a multi-generation to set a standard and to fulfill it corporately. Isaiah 49:22-23 says:

> *Thus says the Lord GOD:*
> *"Behold, I will lift My hand in an oath to the nations,*
> *And set up My standard for the peoples;*
> *They shall bring your sons in their arms,*
> *And your daughters shall be carried on their shoulders;*
> *Kings shall be your foster fathers,*
> *And their queens your nursing mothers;*
> *They shall bow down to you with their faces to the earth,*
> *And lick up the dust of your feet.*
> *Then you will know that I am the LORD,*
> *For they shall not be ashamed who wait for Me."*

What a wonderful promise! *Whatever* is going on around us, even in the midst of raging battles, God speaks to us and says He will be a banner and will set a standard for His people.

It's time to claim our territory — our families, our churches, our cities, our nation, and this emerging generation — for God. And God wants us to celebrate Him. He's called us to be like the leper who returned to thank Jesus for his healing. God wants us to have an attitude of gratitude no matter what we may be going through.

Characteristics of a Standard-Bearer

I believe God is calling people of the emerging generation to be standard bearers who say, "We will not be moved." Those who bear a standard are those who cast a vision and raise it high for others to follow. They not only *raise* a standard, they *set* the standard, based on the Word of God. A standard of character is what attracts the very power and presence of God, empowering standard-bearers to be leaders in this generation.

First: God is looking for leaders of *humility, holiness, honor* and *honesty*. These are individuals willing to walk in the fear of the Lord and a spirit of brokenness. Proverbs 22:4 says: *"By humility and the fear of the Lord are riches, honor and life."* Only the presence of God can bring personal and corporate transformation. We need standard bearers in this generation who will walk in the attributes that attract His presence and favor.

The Book of Esther is a beautiful story of how just one moment of favor from the king turned around a whole national disaster. In the same way, one moment of favor from the King of Kings and Lord of Lords can turn our circumstances around instantly. God can do in a moment what it takes years for us to do on our own.

Second: God wants to raise up leaders who have *a strong personal prayer life*. What we do behind closed doors when no one else can see determines the power of God or lack of it in our lives in public. Who are we in private?

Standard bearers are called to a higher consecration. The high calling of God is not about men ordaining us but about God setting us apart. "Ordination" is about men recognizing what God has already done, and with that recognition comes greater responsibility. "Though others may, we may not." God is calling us to judge ourselves with a greater judgment.

A strong prayer life and being the same person of consecration and holiness in private as we are in public are God's desires for His standard bearers.

Third: God wants leaders with a *Kingdom vision* who can see things beyond themselves. Life is not about personal feelings—it's about the bigger picture. We don't have time to get caught up in what is going on around us because our battle is not with flesh and blood. We need something real and tangible inside of us to keep us going. We cannot live on momentum alone, because eventually momentum runs out. Passion without principles and purpose will not sustain us.

Passion without principles and purpose will not sustain us.

Fourth: God is looking for leaders of *perseverance*, those who keep focused on the vision with persistence and courage. When we get discouraged, we can compromise God's intended purposes and vision for our lives. We need to remind ourselves of the promises of God, especially when we go through challenges, because holding on to His prophetic promise keeps us focused on our purposes and our destinations. We cannot allow ourselves to be distracted by our challenges. As Ed Cole used to say, "Winners only see where they're going, not what they're going through."

We need to be like Joshua and Caleb, who did not look *at* the circumstances but looked *past* them. The other ten spies came back reporting, "It is as God says it is—but the giants are so big that we're like grasshoppers in our own sight" (Numbers 13:33, paraphrased). If we see ourselves as grasshoppers, so do the giants. But Joshua and Caleb were able to see the finish line and hold on to the promises of God. God has given us prophetic words we must not lose, regardless of what we see. He has already given us a promise of victory and not defeat. He says *you* raise a standard, and I will empower you to fight and win!

When we abide in God's holiness, nothing can come against us. He is our banner and rallying point, our victory. It's not about what we see—it's about Who we know and Who lives in us!

True Worshippers

Our giftings and abilities can only take us so far, but God can take us places that seem impossible.

There is one more crucial way to attract God's favor, and that is *worshipping Him in spirit and in truth*. Worship is the foundation for attracting the manifest presence of the Lord. When we are in God's presence, in that holy and consecrated place, our communion with Him is completely undivided. We are so taken with God's power, all we can say is, "Holy, holy, holy is the name of God!" We are in awe of God. And in that place, we see we are undone and we recognize His abounding grace.

In that place of undivided worship, we receive our commission to go out with His authority (Isaiah 6:5-9). Our giftings and abilities can only take us so far, but God can take us places that seem impossible.

Courage Begets Courage

In the movie *The Patriot*, the Minutemen were running away from the British Army in fear. Their standard, the American flag, had been dropped to the ground. In a moment of personal courage, Mel Gibson's character grabbed the flag in the midst of the retreating army and waved it proudly as he advanced toward the enemy. That one act of courage brings hope and strength to the other soldiers as they, too, find the courage to face the enemy, reminding them they were part of a battle and destiny much bigger than themselves.

Likewise, in the Battle of Iwo Jima, amidst the bullets and the carnage, five American marines and one Navy corpsman grabbed the American flag, raised it, and set it in the ground as if to say, "We will not be defeated!" The moment was immortalized in a Pulitzer Prize-winning photograph that speaks a thousand words even today as an act of courage and inspiration to us all.

In the same way, this emerging generation will lead a movement of purity, passion, and purpose in the name of the Lord. They are a generation unashamed of the Gospel and unwilling to compromise the True Standard, the Word of God.

It's a standard they are willing to *raise* high for all to see.

> *God is urgently calling His standard bearers to assemble and lead multi-generations into their prophetic destinies.*

They *set* the standard firmly and send forth a message, "We will not be moved."

And as they *live* the standard, they attract the manifest presence of God and are endued with His power.

As they move forth in courage, others are encouraged and inspired to persevere in the battle.

Who Will Go?

God is urgently calling His standard bearers to assemble and lead multi-generations into their prophetic destinies. So how can we be part of the movement that raises the standard high? How can we be leaders who have the courage to fight? How can we participate in a generation-spanning movement, culminating in the fulfillment of the prayers and words spoken by prophets of old?

We must walk in humility, holiness, honor, and honesty, in a consecrated place in God's presence through intimate prayer, praise, and worship. We must have persevering and courageous hearts to hold those standards high no matter what giants or circumstances may stand in our way. And we must live beyond ourselves and become part of a bigger vision.

Who among us will raise that standard and be that standard bearer, doing whatever it takes to attract the favor and presence of God? Who will walk forth endued with power from the Source Giver? As John Wesley, the great revivalist of the 18th century, said, "Give me 100 men who fear nothing but God and hate nothing but sin, and we'll change the world."

Are you ready to be part of a multi-generational movement that raises a standard and changes the world?

13

Salty Christians

Salty Christians

We have all heard it said that you can lead a horse to water but you can't make him drink. This may be true, but you can give the horse enough salt to make him thirsty. If we truly become the salt of the earth, as God has called us to be, we will create thirst in those around us.

> *"Then the men of the city said to Elisha, 'Please notice, the situation of this city is pleasant, as my lord sees; but the water is bad, and the ground barren.' And he said, 'Bring me a new bowl, and put salt in it.' So they brought it to him. Then he went out to the source of the water, and cast in the salt there, and said, 'thus says the Lord: 'I have healed this water; from it there shall be no more death or barrenness "*
>
> *-2 Kings 2:19-21*

In this story, the water in the land is bitter and poisoned and people are dying from it. But when Elisha goes to the source of the water and puts salt in it, the water is healed and the barrenness is gone.

Salt is a seasoning and a preservative, and it also has medicinal values. Likewise, this emerging generation has learned to become the salt of the earth, bringing healing, life, and flavor to a world of barrenness and death. Like salt, they can melt and tenderize hearts that are hardened to the Gospel. They're "salty Christians."

A generation who knows how to forgive and even honor those who have hurt them will be released into their futures and become the salt of the earth.

Regardless of their pasts, the words spoken against them, circumstances that have crushed them, and prejudices raised against them, they hold fast to God's true revelation of their identity in Him. A generation who knows how to forgive and even honor those who have hurt them will be released to their futures and become the salt of the earth.

They will be a generation that will make others thirsty for God, and those who are hungry and thirsty for righteousness *will* be filled.

God is Giving Us a Wake-Up Call

You and I have a great opportunity, even a responsibility, to impact lives with the Gospel and to impact this emerging generation by helping guide them out of the wilderness. Time is running out, and there is a sense of urgency in the spiritual realm.

I once had a dream that God used to illustrate this to me in a sobering way. In the dream, I was staying in a hotel and had an urgent meeting beginning at 7:00 the next morning. I called the front desk and requested a 5:30 a.m. wake-up call, allowing plenty of time to make the meeting.

The Lord showed me in advance that this 7 a.m. meeting was very critical. If I made the meeting and spoke the word of the Lord into the situation, multitudes would be spared. If I missed the appointment and the word of the Lord was not spoken in due season, multitudes would go into catastrophic danger. I took this very seriously.

To ensure I would be on time, I used my standard back-up plan and set my alarm clock to ring a few minutes after the wake-up call. At 5:30 a.m., the phone rang. "Mr. Stringer, this is your wake-up call." I said thank you and hung up the phone. I thought, *I have a few more minutes before the alarm clock will ring. I'm going back to sleep. I'm exhausted.* I lay back down.

Then the alarm clock rang. I was still tired, so I pushed the snooze button.

Just a few more minutes and I'll be ready to get up.

The alarm rang again, and I pushed the snooze button again — I did this several times. When I finally woke up, it was after 7 a.m.!

The Lord spoke to my heart in the dream and said, "Because you missed that meeting, multitudes are now in danger. You didn't speak the word in season at that meeting, and now you are responsible."

I woke up from that dream with a soberness and fear of the Lord. I recognized the potential we have in this season to kick-start revival. But for that to happen, we have to wake from our sleep. We cannot be distracted. We cannot look to the left or to the right. We must fine tune our ears and hear what the Spirit of the Lord is saying. God is giving us a wake-up call.

God wants us to arise! The Lord wants to bring a sustainable awakening that is exponential and transcends every denomination and ethnic background. This move of God will bridge the generations. The anointing of the older generation will be poured out exponentially on the younger generation.

In the midst of world-wide turmoil and shaking, an army of young

> *The Lord wants to bring a sustainable awakening that is exponential and transcends every denomination and ethnic background.*

people is being released. Many will emerge as full-time, volunteer laborers for God's kingdom (Psalm 110:2-3). They are determined to make a difference. God will enable them to impact every element of their culture and subculture.

You and I have a strategic role in this process. Each generation has something to give. The wisdom of the older joined with the zeal and passion of youth will impact many with the Gospel. God's intention is to bring revival in an exponential way through a young generation, and we are to stand with them.

He is calling the Bride to prepare herself and restore an altar of worship for the ark of His presence.

What we do *together* is critical. God intends to release a massive move of His Spirit. He is calling the Bride to prepare herself and restore an altar of worship for the ark of His presence. When all that can be shaken is shaken, God wants His church to be an ark of refuge, a place to which people can run.

The ark of God's presence will rest in the church who has prepared herself. She has been diligent and will be found spotless and blameless. She will not be a cosmetic bride, compensating on the outside for a lack on the inside. Nor will she be an institution. With depth of character, she will be prepared for the Lord's presence. There, God will dwell.

On the Edge of Eternity

Satan failed to accomplish his task when he killed the innocent children in Moses' and Jesus' day. Now he is targeting this emerging prophetic generation. He wants to stop them early on so they won't fulfill their purpose. What can you and I do to help?

It's time for the children to come forth, and we must give them strength. It's time for the church to be birthed, and we must persevere through the delivery!

God's intended purpose is to bring a great awakening to and through this generation. We must awaken from our slumber and heed the Lord's call in this crucial hour for our nation and the world.

The bottom line is this: *God is doing something!* We don't need to fear what is happening but to embrace it and take it one bit at a time. We must be willing to go with the change. We need each other. We simply cannot do it alone. There is a treasure in this generation, and we must find it.

God's intended purpose is to bring a great awakening to and through this generation.

At this very moment, millions are in the crucial valley of decision, living on the edge of eternity. We have a responsibility to bring them through the valley and to bring them to the cross.

The time is now!

Part V

Who's Your Daddy *Now?*

14

Dougie, Fix It?

Dougie, Fix It?

The burdens of the world are too much to bear alone, yet with the empowerment from the Holy Spirit and the tangible expression of the Heavenly Father, we can present Him to others. If we can give people hope and direct them to the Father, He'll move by His Spirit to take care of the rest. We must return to the Scriptures and look to the God of *all* generations and *all* nations, who seals us with the Spirit of Adoption through the acceptance of Jesus Christ as Lord and Master.

I met with a pastor and his wife from Brazil who were visiting Houston and praying about planting a church here. They told me about their ministry to street kids in Rio and how they once asked a seven-year-old boy who his father was. The child answered with what they believed was the name of a demonic spirit.

What a tragedy! Because these children don't know who their fathers are, they adopt the names of demons. But because of the tangible expression of Christ from this couple and those they labor with, this little orphan boy now answers that same question with the name of Jesus. He has become part of the emerging prophetic generation, adopted into the family of the Heavenly Father through faith in the Son.

As John the Baptist was anointed and empowered to usher in the arrival of Christ, the emerging generation is anointed to usher in a great outpouring of God's presence in preparation for Christ's return. And just as God wants to adopt them, so, too, does the enemy desire to be their counterfeit father.

Every battle in history with the saints of God has been a battle through which Satan challenged God's authority.

Sam, a marketplace minister in Hollywood, says, "Every battle in history with the saints of God has been a battle through which satan challenged God's authority." In effect, he does so by presenting the question, "Who's your daddy?" If he can successfully remove our children's biological fathers, he stands a better chance of usurping God's role of Father, as well. We must not be negligent in exposing him as a counterfeit.

Dougie, Fix It!

My sister Jeanne and my brother Kenny are nine and ten years younger than I. Growing up, I helped take care of them so I became like a father figure to them.

When we were young, Jeanne slipped away from the house one day while I was at school. The police found her blocks away and were driving her up and down the streets to help her find our house when my mom spotted her in the police car. "Mommy! Mommy!" she cried when she saw my mother. It turns out she was looking for her big brother Dougie, so she sneaked out the front gate and headed for the Little League field where she had watched me play ball. The field was a couple of miles from the house and across a busy highway! When she was older, she put all my sports trophies in a pillow case and slept with them. One time she took them with her to school for show-and-tell.

I took Jeanne and Kenny everywhere I went. They looked up to me and wanted to be with me all the time. When they were scared, they slept in my room. And whenever something went wrong, they would often bring the problem to me, hoping I could fix it.

In 1994, we found out my stepfather (their biological father) had just been diagnosed with military-related lung cancer, and we drove from Houston to Waco to see him. My little sister by then was not only a grown adult but also a wife and a mom. I'll never forget how she looked at me that day in the car—distraught at the thought of losing her father to cancer—and said, "Dougie, fix it."

I was seized at that moment with an overwhelming sense of responsibility and the ache of not knowing what to do. I had been so often used by the Lord all over the world, and here I was now, wanting so much to be there for my little brother and sister—yet feeling so helpless. This time, Dougie couldn't fix it.

But our Heavenly Father can fix any situation, though it's not always the way we want Him to. My step-dad passed away six months later, but when he left us, he went to be with Jesus.

Years before, I had shared the Gospel with my step-dad and had given him a Bible. He had professed to know Christ at one time after I was able to lead him in a salvation prayer. But though he was no longer an atheist, and I rejoiced in that, he still had struggles and challenges in his new-found journey. His illness brought him to a place of really looking at all the Lord had spoken to him in the previous few years. During those six months, we were assured he had totally given Lordship to Jesus, and so we are also secure in knowing he is rejoicing in heaven.

In addition to Jeanne and Kenny, I have a half-sister, Judy, who was born to my dad when he remarried after he and my mom divorced. When I met Judy, I was already grown and she was in elementary school. Judy didn't want to take my trophies to show-and-tell, she wanted to take *me*! It was such a novel thing for her to learn she had an older brother who was Japanese.

Years after our father passed away, Judy called and left a message on my voice mail at work. Our ministry at one time had partnered with CBN to distribute 500,000 copies of *The Book of Hope* throughout the city. She had come across one and saw our "Somebody Cares" stamp on the inside cover. She had been praying to Jesus but still could not to come to grips with the loss of our father. She was his little girl, and she adored him. "I just don't understand why Dad had to die," she said tearfully in her message. She could not understand why God didn't "fix it."

But in reality, He *did* fix it! Dad had given his life to Christ, and he is now with Jesus in heaven. And even though I go through moments of missing them, there remains a supernatural peace that surpasses all understanding in knowing my biological father, my stepfather, and my mother are all dancing with Jesus! I know we will meet again and rejoice together for eternity at the throne of the Lord because we all have the same Daddy *NOW*!

A God of Redemption

I praise God for His redemptive power and how He allowed me to see it in the life of my dad. There was such beauty in the way he loved and spoiled Judy. She really was "daddy's little girl." God allowed me to see him free from alcohol. And He allowed me to be a part of my dad's salvation experience as he read my books and listened to my teaching tapes. Years later, his wife Margaret would say to me, "If you only knew how proud he was to have you for a son. He just didn't know how to tell you." This difficulty many of us have in expressing ourselves to our spouses, families, and loved ones is a hindrance to our ability to connect with one another. We are not able to express our affirmation, approval, and acceptance. That's why I say now, "Communication is a key to life."

When my step-dad was diagnosed with cancer, I was determined not to miss the last days of his life like I did when I missed that last week of my dad's life. I commuted to Waco often during that time to be with him.

That next six months was a beautiful time of reminiscing and reflection, laughter and tears. He often told us he loved us and asked us to take care of our mom. We realized that even though we'd gone through a lot of dysfunction, we had still been a family, the best we knew how. Even with the challenges we experienced when I was growing up, I realized he really had been a father to me because he was there for me—at least he *came* to my games. Even if he didn't know how to express it, I knew he loved me and was proud to consider me a son.

We realized that even though we'd gone through a lot of dysfunction, we had still been a family, the best we knew how.

In his latter years, I had seen God's redemption once again as my stepfather poured his life and his love into Jeanne's and Kenny's children. Even though, because of his own challenges, he had not always known how to be a good father to us when we were growing up, he was a very good grandfather. He would take my mom and the kids camping and fishing and on other outings. He spent so much time with them.

Our God is a God of redemption and a God of reconciliation. As our fatherless generations walk through their journeys without the affirmation, approval, and acceptance of their earthly fathers and mothers, it is important to give our parents the grace to change when God begins to move in their lives. Just as we desire for others not to hold us to our pasts, we must not hold them to their pasts, but to acknowledge who they have become or who they *can* become in Christ. This is one of the ways we honor God by honoring our parents, as we choose, like Shem and Japheth did in the case of Noah, to cover their nakedness.

The Prayers Of A Child

And He said to them, "Why did you seek Me? Did you not know that I must be about My Father's business?
                                                    -Luke 2:49

At the young age of 12, Jesus knew who His Father was. We, too, must have that same kind of faith or we will never enter the fullness of the Kingdom.

Assuredly, I say to you, whoever does not receive the king-dom of God as a little child will by no means enter it
                                    -Mark 10:15, Luke 18:17

Before Jeanne was born, I had asked God for a little sister and He answered my prayer. "I promise I'll teach her all about You," I had said to Him. A year later, my mother was expecting another baby, so I prayed again. "God, you gave me a sister, and I am so thankful. Now if you give me a brother, I'll teach him about You, too." He answered my prayer again and Kenny was born, but this time there were complications.

Kenny came four months early. He had pneumonia and a hernia and had to have two operations on his eyes. It was questionable if he would even live. Doctors said if he did live, he would be "slow" or maybe even a "vegetable." I sat in the car outside the hospital and cried to the Lord on behalf of my little brother.

"Jesus, please! You gave me a sister a year ago, now you gave me a brother. The doctors say he might not live, but I don't believe that. Please make him healthy!"

Once again, God heard the petitions of a little boy who didn't even know that much about Him. Kenny not only survived, but overcame all those challenges, barriers, and obstacles to become a sharp, intelligent young man. He went to a technical institute, then he joined the Navy to follow in the footsteps of his father. Later, he moved to Houston and worked in banking.

Kenny went through a difficult and painful divorce that left some deep emotional wounds that have compounded certain challenges and issues he is going through today. His children now live out of state, and because of his desire to see them more often, he left his job in banking to become a flight attendant. He called me after one of his trips just to leave a message that he got to spend time with them on one four-day lay-over near their home.

A few weeks prior to that, he had called me after returning from one of his first trips with the airline.

"What are you doing?" he asked.

"I'm having dinner with friends. Are you hungry?"

"No, I already ate. I just wanted to talk to you."

"We'll wait for you," I said. "Come on over."

I hung up the phone and said to my friends, "He wants me to see him in his flight attendant's uniform."

Sure enough, Kenny came straight from the airport so big brother Doug could see him in his uniform! Even now, he still looks to me as a father figure to give him affirmation, acceptance, and approval.

In their early years, I taught Jeanne and Kenny about God, but in my teen-age years I departed from His ways and was not faithful to keep the promise I made to Him so many years earlier. For a season I left home and was estranged from my family. That's when Jeanne began sleeping with my sports trophies. The day she took them with her to school for show-and-tell, I told her to wait for me after school and I would meet her there. She sat on the curb for hours, but I never showed up. There were so many times I failed them.

Yet God was faithful in spite of it all, and He watched out for them. My prayer for Kenny, Jeanne, and Judy continues to be that they would grow into fullness of relationship with their Heavenly Father, who can love them in a way no parent or no big brother ever can. He will never leave them or forsake them. He will *never* fail them.

Who's YOUR Daddy Now?

When Jesus taught the disciples to pray using the word "Father," He knew the power of coming to God, knowing God's position as Father and ours as His children. Likewise, when those around us ask, "Who's your daddy?" we must know in our heart of hearts that the Divine Creator is also a Father who loves us, accepts us, liberates us, and empowers us, no matter who we are or where we've come from.

We must know in our heart of hearts that the Divine Creator is also a Father who loves us, accepts us, liberates us, and empowers us, no matter who we are or where we've come from.

Are you from the former generation who did not get an understanding of how to be parents because they did not have that role properly modeled in their own lives?

Are you from the emerging generation who are looking for spiritual fathers to bless them, release them into their destinies, and give them approval, affirmation, and acceptance?

Are you one of those "camels" wandering in the wilderness who has never come to a knowledge of Jesus as Savior?

No matter who you are, the Father waits for you with open arms. All the riches of God await you in His presence. He has an inheritance for you, He has a destiny for you, and He wants to bring you into His family through the Spirit of Adoption. All you need to do is receive Him, by faith in His Son.

One night I was in New England preparing to preach the next day. When I checked my voice mail before going to bed, I discovered a message from Jeanne. One of her friends who had been expecting a baby had just miscarried. As she was grieving for her friend's loss, she began reflecting on her own family and the many ways God has blessed her. She called me just to let me know she was thinking about me.

"I don't know if you can understand the impact you've had on my life. The earliest memories I have are of you taking care of me and protecting me," she said. "Other people know you as Pastor Doug, but I know you as 'Dougie.' I am so blessed to have two wonderful brothers who love me. No one loves you like I do. You introduced me to my Father in heaven, and I am so thankful for that." Because I was a father figure to my little brother and sister, I can now remind them who their Daddy is now. There is a God in heaven, and He loves them. He rocks! He can fix it! All they need to know is they can turn to Him, and He will be there for them.

We cannot change our pasts, but the choices we make today will affect our futures.

Just as I would say that to my brother and my sisters, I say the same to each of you. Are you willing to receive Him as your Father through the Spirit of Adoption?

In light of our generations being part of the corporate fatherless generations, we must ask ourselves the question, "Who is my daddy?"

In our past choices, we have brought hurt or disappointment to others. We have experienced pain and dysfunction. We cannot change our pasts, but the choices we make today will affect our futures. We can choose now to look upon our Heavenly Father, who can be tangible to us. We can call Him "Abba." He is the one who will never disappoint us, who will never forsake us. And we know Him through His son Jesus, because to know the Son is to know the Father.

Let Him embrace you with His tangible presence. Know that you are fully accepted, affirmed, and approved, and you have an inheritance waiting for you. Receive the Father's blessing.

Who's *YOUR* Daddy now?

END-NOTES

Chapter 3:

1. Jack Neff, "News You Can Use On Your Bottom Line," Comair *Navigator*, February/March 2002, page 3.
2. Wikipedia Encyclopedia, www.wikepedia.org, 2005.
3. Battlecry. May 2006 <http://www.battlecry.com>.
4. Doug Stringer, *The Fatherless Generation*, Destiny Image Publishers, 1994, page 2.
5. Jack Graham, *Father Knows Best CD album*, Power Point Ministries, www.jackgraham.org.
6. Jeremy Del Rio, *Commit to the Fatherless this Father's Day*, www.pastors.com, July 2006
7. Reprinted by permission. *Rachel's Tears*, Beth Nimmo and Darrell Scott, 2000. Thomas Nelson Inc. Nashville, Tennessee. All rights reserved. pp. 36, 55.
8. Tim Clinton, American Association of Christian Counselors, 2006.

Chapter 4:

1. Doug Stringer, "Pray Until Something Happens," *Charisma*, March 1999.
2 & 3. Jeffery L. Sheler, "Faith in America," *U.S. News and World Report*, May 6, 2002, p. 45.

Chapter 5:

1. Doug Stringer, *The Fatherless Generation*, Destiny Image Publishers, 1994, page 15.
2. Mission America Coalition Update, July 20, 2006.

Chapter 6:

1 Joan of Arc material from various historical sources, paraphrased by Doug Stringer

Chapter 7:

1. "A Letter from Pete Furler," *The Purple Book*, Every Nations Productions, 2004.
2. Peter Ferrara, "What is an American?" in *The National Review*, September 2001.
3. Adrienne S. Gaines, "The Joshua Generation?" *Catalyst* magazine, Spring/Summer 2001, p.1.

Chapter 8:

1. James Boswell story from various historical sources, paraphrased by Doug Stringer.
2. "From Boomers to Zoomers," Continental Airlines Magazine, June 2001, p. 26.
3. New Choices Magazine: Reader's Digest, November 2001
4. Tim Smart, "Not Acting Their Age," *U.S. News and World Report*, June 4, 2001, p. 56.

Chapter 9:

1. Reuben Morgan, "You Said" from *Open the Eyes of My Heart*, Hillsong Music Australia, 1998.

About the Author

Dr. J. Doug Stringer, Founder
Turning Point Ministries International/Somebody Cares America-International

Dr. J. Doug Stringer is founder and president of Turning Point Ministries International, which birthed an international movement known as Somebody Cares, a network of organizations impacting their communities through unified grassroots efforts. Doug began identifying community needs through his work in the inner-city of Houston, Texas in 1981. The collaborative network has grown rapidly and now impacts cities around the world.

A licensed pastoral counselor and ordained minister, Doug holds a Ph.D. in leadership and human development from Logos University, along with a pastoral certificate in practical ministry from Regent University. He is recognized for his contributions in both secular and sacred arenas. Doug received congressional recognition for the work of Somebody Cares in 2001 and the Barbara Jordan Leadership Award in 1995. He has served with the Houston area Council on Gangs and as a Community Relations Consultant for Houston Police Department's Community Outreach Division and currently serves on HPD's Youth Police Advisory Council. Doug is co-founder of Global Compassion Network (GCN), a network of worldwide compassion ministries, and serves as a board member or advisor for a variety of organizations, including: Asian Task Force, World Blessing Foundation, Sentinel Group with George Otis Jr., Mission Houston, Mission America, Youth-Reach Houston, and the Governor of Texas' One Star Foundation.

Somebody Cares has implemented several city-wide strategies now duplicated in cities across the nation, including a mentoring program for youth known as Youth Guidance Consultants. Somebody Cares also developed an anti-gang and at-risk youth intervention handbook, which has been utilized by the Houston Police Department. Back-to-school programs and benevolent aid during the holiday season known as Holiday of Hope have been integral parts of Somebody Care's efforts. In addition, Somebody Cares initiated an awareness campaign for potential adoptive parents known as Hope in Houston. Because of the ministry's extensive network of relationships throughout the U.S. and abroad, Somebody Cares emerged in 2005 as a leader in "rapid response" to disaster relief, beginning with the tsunami in Southeast Asia and continuing with Hurricanes Katrina and Rita. The ministry's work was recognized in *Charisma* and *Outreach* magazines and featured on American Family Radio, Moody Broadcasting, and www.crosswalk.com.

Doug is the author of the books *It's Time to Cross the Jordan, The Fatherless Generation, Somebody Cares,* and *Born to Die.* He is published in numerous magazines and websites including: *The Houston Chronicle, New Man, Charisma, Decision Magazine, National Religious Broadcasters Magazine, Christian Single* and www.crosswalk.com. Doug is a frequent presenter at workshops such as "Save Our Children," "Seminar of Youth Problems," "A Forum on Racial & Ethnic Tensions in Schools," as well as Cultural Awareness forums. He is also a sought after speaker at religious, political, educational and civic gatherings.

As an Asian-American, Doug is considered a bridge-builder and ambassador of reconciliation amongst various ethnic and religious groups. From police departments, congressmen, to international government officials, Doug shares a key concept: Working together we can be more effective in our community efforts.

For more information call 713-621-1498
or visit www.dougstringer.com

New Releases

&

GateKeeper Recommended Reading

JOHN LOUIS MURATORI

RICH CHURCH

Pr Church

UNLOCK the *SECRETS* of CREATING *WEALTH*
and *HARNESS* the POWER of *MONEY*
To *INFLUENCE* EVERYTHING

ISBN 0-9704753-1-4
Hard Cover

Rich Church Poor Church **is the most comprehensive wealth-building book on the market.**

Finally, a unique and insightful book about the controversial topic of wealth building. This book will clarify the issue like none other — it is truly in a league of its own. John Muratori chronicles the history of both God and prosperity, and Biblical economics.

———————————— Topics ————————————

- The History of God & Prosperity
- The Twelve Biblical Laws of Wealth Creation
- Wealth Transference
- A Comprehensive Exposition on the Transference of Wealth from both a Social Economic and Biblical Economic Perspective
- The Superiority of Biblical Wisdom Concerning Wealth and Finance

- How and Why the Church Has Been Deceived to Eliminate the Message of Wealth and Prosperity
- Unlocking the Wealth Building Secrets of Judaism
- Answering the age old question: Why Do The Wicked Prosper and How it Relates to the Readers Personal Sphere of Influence

The priceless insights are guaranteed to move every reader to a fresh level of empowerment and financial liberation.

Written in an informative easy to read style, the emerging generation will quickly grasp this invaluable knowledge. It is a book parents will give to their children to equip them for Biblical prosperity.

Not just a theoretical treatise, but a practical blueprint for financial influence destined to liberate every single reader.

Just the information of the twelve biblical laws of wealth creation would be enough for the reader to be enriched beyond measure.

These principles are trans-generational. It's scriptural message is universal and can be transferred to any culture or country in the world.

The incredible adventure and inestimable wealth of *Rich Church Poor Church* awaits you!

Cover Me in the Day of Battle
By Bishop Bart Pierce

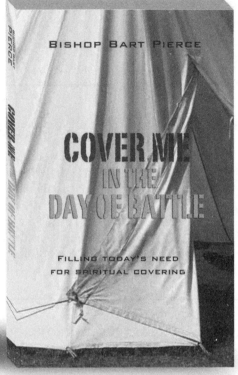

ISBN 0-977689-21-2

Because life is full of daily battles.

Why do good Christian soldiers — pastors, leaders, intercessors, and others — lose some of these battles? Is it possible that they fail to reach their greatest potential because they go to battle without the covering of a spiritual father?

In this day of do-it-yourselfism, Bishop Bart Pierce says it's time to address our need for fathers — both spiritual and natural. It's God's desire and the groan of the world for mature sons to come forth.

Fathers, arise now, and raise up sons. Sons, arise, and get your heads covered, and let's go to battle under the covering of God and our fathers Then the curse of fatherlessness will be broken, and sons will turn to fathers and fathers will turn to sons, so that the Church can be the force God created it to be.

The Bribe of Great Price
By Bishop Bart Pierce

Uncover the greatest scandal in history

ISBN 0-9704753-5-7

In this masterful book, Bart Pierce exposes the greatest scandal in history. He chronicles the radical plot of supernatural forces to silence the voices of truth. Over two millennia ago, a Roman soldier and *"The Bribe of Great Price"* spawned the greatest cover up in history.

The *Bribe* quietly survived the rise and fall of dictators, parliaments, Kingdoms, Empires, and Nations. In a post-modern era, it openly employs the sciences, political systems, religion and mass media. Due to an elaborate deception, even the Church has aided in this conspiracy. This book is definitely a page-turner for every believer, seeker and conspiracy theorist alike. It is an unforgettable journey!

GATEKEEPER PUBLISHING is expanding its authorship with the launch of our new imprint **'Think Big, little books.'** We are looking for fresh, cutting-edge manuscripts that have a relevant message for this hour.

If you would like to submit your manuscript to our acquisitions department, visit us today at **www.gatekeeperpublishing.com**

Are you a published author trying to make a living, writing books?

Then consider joining the GateKeeper family of authors. Be a part of a company setting new industry standards. We commit aggressive marketing budgets to every project and give our authors the highest royalties in the trade.

Whatever your situation, GateKeeper can offer you numerous options to suite your specific needs. We offer a full range of services including:

- ✄ Complete "book publishing" - from concept to completion
- ✄ Innovative Graphics, and full cover design services
- ✄ Audio Book Productions
- ✄ Foreign Language book production, transcriptions and more

If you would like to see our full range of services, or info on submitting your manuscript, please visit our website.

www.gatekeeperpublishing.com